# HELPING TEENS
# WORK THROUGH GRIEF

# HELPING TEENS
# WORK THROUGH GRIEF

## Mary Kelly Perschy, M.S.

**ACCELERATED DEVELOPMENT**

*A member of the Taylor & Francis Group*

| USA | Publishing Office | Accelerated Development<br>A member of the Taylor & Francis Group<br>325 Chestnut Street, Suite 800<br>Philadelphia, PA 19106<br>Tel: (215) 625-8900<br>Fax: (215) 625-2940 |
| --- | --- | --- |
| | Distribution Center | Accelerated Development<br>A member of the Taylor & Francis Group<br>7625 Empire Drive<br>Florence, KY 41042<br>Tel: (800) 634-7064<br>Fax: (800) 248-4724 |
| UK | | Taylor & Francis<br>27 Church Road<br>Hove<br>E. Sussex BN3 2FA<br>Tel: +44 (0) 1273 207411<br>Fax: +44 (0) 1273 205612 |

**HELPING TEENS WORK THROUGH GRIEF**

1 2 3 4 5 6 7 8 9 0     B R B R     9

This book was set in Times Roman. The editors were Cindy Long and Holly Seltzer. Technical development by Cindy Long. Prepress supervisor was Miriam Gonzalez. Cover design by Ed Atkeson, Berg Design.

A CIP catalog record for this book is available from the British Library.
♾ The paper in this publication meets the requirements of the ANSI Standard Z39.48-1984 (Permanence of Paper)

**Library of Congress Cataloging-in-Publication Data**
Perschy, Mary Kelly
    Helping teens work through grief/Mary Kelly Perschy.
        p.   cm.
    Includes bibliographical references and index.

    1. Grief in adolescence.   2. Bereavement in adolescence.   3. Grief therapy.   4. Group counseling.   5. Teenagers—Counseling of.
    6. Group counseling.   I. Title.
BF724.3.G73P47   1997                                          96-48297
155.9'37'0835—DC21                                            CIP

ISBN 1-56032-558-5 (paper)

# DEDICATION

To those teens
who have shared the turmoil of their grief

and

to those teens who are willing to
enter into that struggle,

that their pain may be healed
and they may experience renewed life

# TABLE OF CONTENTS

**PART C**
**EVALUATION AND FOLLOW-UP**

# LIST OF ACTIVITY SHEETS

# LIST OF FIGURES

# ACKNOWLEDGMENTS

Grateful acknowledgement is made to these authors and publishers for permission to reprint the following:

From *The Courage to Grieve* by Judith Tatelbaum. Copyright © 1980, Judith Tatelbaum, published by HarperCollins Publishers Inc.

From "The Role of School Counselors with Bereaved Teenagers: With and without Peer Support Groups" by Ross Gray in *The School Counselor*. Copyright © 1988, published by American Counseling Association.

From *Grief Counseling and Grief Therapy* by William Worden. Copyright © 1991, used by permission of Springer Publishing Company, Inc., New York 10012.

From *The Focusing Steps* by Edwin M. McMahon and Peter A. Campbell. Copyright © 1991, by Edwin M. McMahon, Ph.D, and Peter A. Campbell, Ph.D., published by Sheed and Ward.

From "No Where to Run" by Katie Williams. From *Bereavement Magazine,* October, 1992, 8133 Telegraph Drive, Colorado Springs, CO 80920.

From *Write Grief: How to Transform Loss with Writing* by Gail Jacobsen. Copyright © 1990, Gail Jacobsen, published by McCormick and Schilling.

From *Mind, Music, and Imagery* by Stephanie Merritt. Copyright © 1996, Stephanie Merritt. Used with permission of Aslan Publishing.

From "Teen Suicide: Source, Signals and Prevention" by Robert Stevenson in *The Dying and Bereaved Teenager* by John Morgan. Copyright © 1990, published by The Charles Press, Publishers, Inc.

# INTRODUCTION

When I first heard Elisabeth Kubler-Ross speak, I was touched by her compassion toward dying persons and their families. This noted expert on the grieving process spoke of grieving persons' depression, helplessness, and anger. She elaborated on family members' anger toward doctors, at the person who died, and especially at God. Kubler-Ross understood me; her words resonated with the turbulent feelings that haunted me for years. That day she gave the audience a special gift—permission to grieve. She also encouraged us to be with grieving persons in a nonjudgmental way.

I had lived under a pall of dark clouds for years, and now the explanation was simple. I never had grieved the death of my mother when I was 16. "Your mother is in a better place. Get on with your life," I was told. "Time heals all."

Time did not heal the pain. For many years I felt like there was a solid rock embedded in my chest, and it pulled me down like an extra dose of gravity. Now I had a name for it— unresolved grief. Over the next few years, I talked about it with a few select companions. The dark clouds parted; the light began to shine through. The pull of that rock had dissipated.

When I completed my graduate degree in counseling, I was drawn into hospice work. I felt that I could help provide what was missing when I was 16: support for grieving teens. Teens no longer would need to feel so isolated as they endured the intensity of their grief and struggled through the grieving process.

As 15-year-old Laurie said, "I thought my feelings were dumb, and I was ashamed of them. Then I came to this group [on working through the grieving process] and realized that others have the same feelings. When I'm with others outside this group, I feel abnormal. Here, I feel more secure. I am a normal grieving person."

This manual is written for adults who are willing to connect with grieving teens, including counselors, trained hospice volunteers, religious youth staff, teachers, and mentors. It is not the final word, but rather a valuable resource that will help adults connect with teens who have experienced losses.

The diverse activities offered in these pages have been used with many teens and have been refined continually over the years. Some of the activities present valuable information about grief and how it can affect people's lives. Other activities provide a structure to enable teens to reflect upon and talk about their individual concerns. Other suggestions address the stress of dealing with the inner turmoil of grief when all the teen really desires is to be a normal adolescent.

This practical book contains the nuts and bolts of setting up a teen group for working through the grieving process. The information also can be adapted for working individually with a teen. Reference sections on teen grief, characteristics of leaders, how to interface effectively with parents, suggestions for follow-up, and how to determine when professional help is needed make this work a valuable asset.

This book is a guide. The special needs of the grieving teens and their willingness to engage in the process determine what actually will occur. Even a well-planned agenda may become secondary to a spontaneous need expressed by one or more participant. Flexibility is essential to engage teens in working through their unique experiences of grief.

As a mental health professional, I value the confidentiality of the teens with whom I work. Therefore, in this book I have used quotes only from a meeting where everyone agreed to waive confidentiality for the purpose of informing the general public about teen grief.

My hope is that this book will encourage adults to reach out and provide a safe place for young grieving persons to be with the turmoil of grief and allow new life to emerge.

I would like to say a special thanks to the many people who encouraged me to write about how to help teens grieve, particularly the following:

the staff and caregivers at Hospice Services of Howard County, Maryland, past and present, who have been sensitive to the needs of grieving teens and children;

members of my writers' group, along with David Dupree, Stephanie Rusk, and Sue and Tom Hartman, for their suggestions in making the manuscript more readable;

Beth Beil, Lori Butkovich, Susan Garner, and John Hayes, who provided valuable support and feedback from a mental health professional perspective;

Ellie Klau, Barbara Taylor, and Ed and Robbie Sabin, for their practical suggestions in making this publication a reality;

Robin Wachur for sharing the memory bead project and Kelley Shannon for the good-bye exercise;

Kathleen Kelly, who created the illustrations and cover art and shared her insights on art and grief;

my brother, Tom, from Kelly Expressions Limited, for my photo and the many photos he has provided over the years;

my husband, Jim, who saw me through the mechanics of word processing to the final printing of the manuscript;

Joe Hollis, Cindy Long, and Jim Morgan, who have been so encouraging as they guided me from manuscript to completed book; and

the many people who offered a word of support.

Finally, I am most grateful for the inspiration of the trusting teens who share their struggles of grief and are courageous enough to move through that pain to a new place of healing.

# CRAZY QUILT: SYMBOL OF GRIEF

Often a grieving person will share in a low voice, "I fell like I'm going crazy." A description of ongoing sadness, outbursts of anger, even surprise at the intensity of the feelings usually follows. A favorite melody or a word from a friend can trigger the many feelings of grief when we least expect.

A crazy quilt, with its undefined, overlapping patterns, resembles the process of grief. A collage of pieces of various textures, the quilt reminds us of special people and events, evoking emotions about earlier days with those we love. No two such quilts are alike.

Just as the creation of a crazy quilt captures the uniqueness of our life experience, so too does the process of grief reflect the special connectedness that we had with our loved one who has died. We move on, yet the memories remain. However, we are challenged to reconcile the fact that our lives have changed.

The purpose of a teen grief group is to support those who are grappling with that change. As they attend to the pain of their loss, the teens continue the healing process and become attuned to the new life that is unfolding.

The particular quilt on the cover of this book symbolizes that movement of grief. As adults support teens in grappling with the many pieces of their lives, they help enable teens to become whole.

# Chapter 1

# TEENS AND THE GRIEVING PROCESS

Teen years are tumultuous enough as young people grapple with the many changes of body, mind, and spirit. A grieving teen has that and much more to process. These concepts are elaborated upon in this chapter as a foundation for understanding the struggle of the grieving teen. The descriptions can assist adults in identifying teens who are grieving.

> "Like childhood, adulthood was a calm sea, but the passage
> between the two periods a stormy one."

Rousseau, *Emile*

## TEEN YEARS: THUNDERSTORMS AND TIGHTROPES

The adolescent years resemble a storm. Adolescence is a time of unpredictability, of turmoil, of not being in control. The changing hormones rage, just like the wild winds of a summer thunderstorm. Like the thunder roaring and the lightning flashing, teen years are filled with outbursts of anger and frustration. A lull may follow. A pause, a taste of equilibrium, may precede the next wave of change.

Sometimes there even may be rainbows. Yes, adolescence is also a time of excitement for teens as they discover new strengths. They push their bodies to new limits in favorite sports. They stretch their minds by arguing every point in discussions. They further explore the mysteries of relationships.

Each change brings an element of newness along with the pain of loss; however, teens can experience the losses without the immediate benefit of the gains. This resembles a trapeze artist who has let go of one bar, hoping the other will be in place. These times are filled with both fear and exhilaration.

When the bar is in place, the fear of anticipation changes quickly into elation. When the rope is not yet in the right place or contact is not made, then teens tumble into the safety net. This temporary setback is both frustrating and embarrassing. Worse, when there is no safety net, isolation, discouragement, and despair can overwhelm them.

- Am I really cool?
- Does he like me anymore?
- Will I get into my first-choice college?
- How can I tell Dad that I racked up his car?
- My friend is threatening to commit suicide. What should I say?
- My mom embarrasses me with her drinking.
- I failed the test miserably.

These lows alternate with exuberant highs.

- I scored the winning points for the basketball team.
- I made the cheerleading squad.
- He invited me to the prom!
- I got the scholarship.
- I can hardly wait 'til the rock concert.
- I passed my driver's test.

"Remember, the goal of adolescence is to become free of parental influence," my friend Elaine claims. The same son who insisted that you be present at each little league game a few years ago now may refuse to walk through the mall with you fearing that you may embarrass him by speaking too loudly. After ignoring your presence, he may hand you a sweatshirt and shorts and then expect you to pay for them!

Anthony E. Wolf (1991) described this ambivalence humorously in his book, *Get out of My Life, but First Could You Drive Me and Cheryl to the Mall: A Parent's Guide to the New Teenager.* Recall the safety net. Teens think somewhat like this: "I want to walk the tightrope. I might need you, but please don't fuss if I fall. I'm already too embarrassed about messing up."

The adolescent moves from simplicity to sophistication, dependence to independence or, better yet, interdependence, forming a set of beliefs and values that will define this new person. It is a time filled with challenge, excitement, and success, interspersed with awkwardness and defeat, moving through this all-important passage to adulthood.

An important task of adults is to help teens achieve a balanced and steady growth in spite of their ambivalent, and at times unpleasant, behavior. With the help of caring adults, even teens who face the devastating loss of a parent, sibling, or friend can survive, heal, and grow.

## THE PROCESS OF GRIEF

Grief can make you feel crazy. Every emotion is let loose and comes flooding in, eroding any sense of balance. The normal routine of the most stable individual can be disrupted by bursting into tears or being totally distracted by

the pain of loss. There is no shortcut to make the turmoil
disappear. (Perschy, 1989, p. 1)

These words reflected the experiences of eight grieving teens. These teens complained of feeling that they were going crazy—content one moment, in tears the next. Just traveling down the supermarket aisle can trigger an unexpected flow of tears when a 16-year-old spots her dad's favorite cereal. The intensity and unpredictability of it all adds to the frustration of dealing with grief.

The term **grief** describes the healing process, which includes the ups and downs, the adaptations to change, and the numerous small negotiations, bringing a person to a new dimension of life. After years of studying grieving persons, professionals in the medical and mental health fields have formulated some structured ways of looking at what happens.

## Stages of Grief

Elisabeth Kubler-Ross (1969) popularized the idea of the stages of grief in her book, *On Death and Dying.* In her pioneer studies, she noted that dying persons went through periods of denial and isolation, anger, bargaining, depression, and finally an acceptance of their approaching death. These **stages**, as she called them, then were used to describe the process of grief of the friends and relatives after the loved one died. However, this information was used in ways never intended by Kubler-Ross. The stages were not meant to be interpreted as a formula through which each grieving person needed to pass in a consecutive order.

In reality, as people wrestle with their grief, they may experience emotions such as guilt, hatred, fear, frustration, relief, and even a combination of two or more simultaneously. Persons move through the grief process many times for short or long periods of time before they have a sense of equilibrium that Kubler-Ross refers to as **acceptance.**

Alan Wolfelt (1987), director of the Center for Loss & Life Transition, considered the word **reconciliation** more accurate than acceptance. We may never get over our grief, but we are able to come to the realization that the person has died. As we work through the pain, eventually we are capable of redirecting our energy and initiative toward the future.

## Tasks of Grief

Other models of observing grief describe specific **tasks** that a person needs to accomplish in order to move to a state of reconciliation. The mourners' awareness of these tasks can help them participate in a more active way in the process. For leaders of a grief group, a knowledge of the tasks can provide a framework for planning appropriate activities.

William Worden (1991), author of *Grief Counseling and Grief Therapy,* described four tasks of grieving as

to accept the reality of the loss,

to experience the pain of grief,
to adjust to an environment in which the deceased is missing, and
to emotionally relocate the deceased and move on with life (pp. 10, 13, 14, & 16).

**To Accept the Reality of the Loss.** We often hear from the grieving widow of how she catches herself automatically placing a table setting for her deceased spouse. A teen expects his dad to walk through the door a month after he died of a heart attack. The human mind cannot integrate the loss all at once and often plays tricks on us. It takes a while to comprehend the full reality that the person will no longer be present to us physically.

**To Experience the Pain of Grief.** The pain of grief touches many aspects of our being. Many persons have difficulty eating and sleeping. Headaches and stomach pains, tight muscles, and a general susceptibility to physical ailments are very common.

Emotionally, the intensity varies depending upon the depth of the relationship with the person who died, the effect of the loss on everyday living, and the coping ability of the grieving person. "To work through and complete grief means to face our feelings openly and honestly, to express or release our feelings fully, and to tolerate and accept our feelings for however long it takes for the wound to heal" (Tatelbaum, 1980, p. 9).

**To Adjust to an Environment in Which the Deceased Is Missing.** There are some very practical tasks that need to be performed in families. When a parent dies, who will cook the meals, do the laundry, take out the trash, or drive the car pools? As the family members struggle to take over these roles, the frustration level often increases.

Grieving persons also need to adjust to a new sense of self. People are defined by those around them. When a parent or someone very close to a teen dies, it may affect how the teen perceives himself or herself. Who could replace the listening parent, the one who made the teen feel special? Who can provide the safety net as the teen wrestles with the normal developmental tasks of adolescence? As the teen asks "Who am I?" and "What do I want to become?", who will accompany the search?

The death of a loved one can disrupt a survivor's sense of the world. This is particularly challenging for the teen who already is searching for meaning in life. Faith issues can help or hinder the process. Someone who blocks out a higher being as irrelevant for allowing a person to die may have lost a means of support. Others may find solace and comfort in their spiritual beliefs.

A caring adult can be extremely helpful if a teen allows that person to accompany him or her through these important issues.

**To Emotionally Relocate the Deceased and Move on with Life.** The pain of loss may never be totally gone. Grieving persons can be encouraged to recall the events shared with the deceased and to commemorate the life of that person through ritual in order to eventually lessen the intense emotional attachment. The teen-in-grief may need to regrieve the loss at celebrations or rites of passage. One daughter may miss her mom as she shops for her prom dress; another daughter may miss her dad in later years as she walks down the aisle with her uncle on her wedding day. A son may feel a letdown at graduation as he sees other dads excited over their sons' accomplishments.

Yet, in a normal grief journey, the mourner's emotions have moved from an exaggerated intensity in relation to the deceased to a more integrated state. The person may more easily direct energy toward others. A reconciliation of the loss continues to take place. Life has renewed meaning and purpose.

In chapter 8, Learning about Grief, is a section on "Helps in Moving through Your Grief." The suggestions can help teens reflect on these tasks in relation to their own lives.

## THE GRIEVING TEEN

Life for the teen-in-grief is complex. The emotional turmoil that follows the death of someone close can be unnerving for even the most secure teen. The scariness of the intense mood swings makes some teens question their sanity. The guilt for wishing for the quick death of a pain-stricken parent can weigh heavily on a teen. The intense anger at medical personnel, meddling relatives, and at the person who has died defies logical thinking. The constant ache of loss makes one wonder, "Will I ever feel better?"

The grieving teen must wrestle with the profound changes and intense feelings of adjusting to both adolescence and loss. Some teens have a network of friends to help sort these feelings and these issues; others are not as fortunate. Lisa, a 9th-grader whose dad had died, explained, "My friends would probably think I was weird for talking about family problems." Another girl admitted that her mom had been her confidant. Since her mom's death, she had no one else with whom to talk.

Often, the grieving teen regrets feeling out of sync with peers. When friends are bubbling about a school dance, a football game, or a new outfit, it is difficult to pick up the enthusiasm when one's own mood is so low. As one girl confided, "When someone starts crying over a broken fingernail or a low grade, I just want to scream."

The isolation of not fitting in, at an age when peers are so important, is a key issue in addressing teen grief.

A study of bereaved teens by Ross Gray from Sunnybrook Medical Center in Toronto, Canada, shows that teenagers who scored higher on a measure of social support were significantly less depressed than were those who scored lower on the same measure. While 34% percent of the parents were helpful to their teens,

> 40% reported that the "most helpful person" in dealing with their loss was a peer. This was true for teenagers who were involved in support groups and for those who were not. Support group participants in this study were much more likely to report that they felt peers understood them after their loss than did other bereaved teenagers (76% versus 8%). (Gray, 1988, p. 187)

Eighty percent of the local health professionals and guidance personnel who responded to a bereavement questionnaire of Hospice Services of Howard County, Maryland, requested that the hospice provide a support group for grieving teens. A local psychologist offered to consult with the leaders.

A teen support group can help a teen keep a balance while moving through the throes of grief. It can give participants the support needed to identify themselves as grieving persons and the permission to work through the pain to move to a more peaceful place of reconciling the loss.

When a peer support group is not available, a grieving teen can be helped by a caring person who is willing to be present for the teen throughout the healing journey of grief.

# PART A
# INITIATING, ORGANIZING, AND LEADING A GROUP

Teachers, spiritual youth workers, guidance counselors, and/or coaches often become aware of a few teens who each have experienced a significant loss. Having recognized these teens, the adults frequently consider gathering them together to provide tangible support and to do so in a group setting.

"Where do we begin?", they may ask. Part A of this book is designed to walk a leader through the initial steps in beginning a group. Chapters 2, 3, and 4 present background material about the value of a group, and the role of leaders and parents in working with grieving teens.

Chapter 5 of Part A introduces the practical dimensions of preparing for a group, including the nuts and bolts of publicity and registration. This chapter concludes with suggestions for the all-important ingredient for any teen gathering—the snacks.

Guidance for how to structure the group is provided in chapter 6. The framework is very flexible, enabling leaders to tailor activities to a particular group, whether it is designed for six or eight weeks. The chapter is divided into three components: the first two meetings, the middle meetings, and the last meeting. The first two meetings are structured, ensuring that the essential preliminary details are included, as well as welcoming activities, introductions, and initial information about grief and how it affects our lives. The middle meetings section is more general, as leaders are encouraged to allow the plans to unfold as particular issues or concerns arise. (Numerous activities are included in Part B of this book. These were developed in response to the real-life struggles described by teens.) Specific suggestions are provided for the last meeting to help teens prepare for one more loss—the loss of the structure the group has provided. The activities focus on providing closure.

# Chapter 2

# THE VALUE OF A GROUP IN DEALING WITH GRIEF

Teens who have had a loved one die refer to "feeling out of sync with the crowd." A grief support group helps lessen that feeling of isolation and enables teens to gain support and understanding from one another. The combination of imparting information about grief and providing an opportunity for sharing makes group guidance an effective model for working with grieving teens.

When asked, "What advice would you give a grieving teen?" Karyn said, "Join a teen grief group to help deal with your feelings." Laurie added with a smile, "Yeah, I thought my feelings were dumb and was ashamed of them. Then I came to this group and realized that others have the same feelings. When I am with others outside this group, I feel abnormal. Here I feel more secure. I am a normal grieving person" (Perschy, 1989, p. 3).

## WHY A GROUP?

A common complaint of bereaved teens is the sense of **isolation** that they experience as they talk with their friends or join with the crowd. Although some friends are willing to listen to the real pain of grief, others just don't know what to do or say and become anxious around any talk of the deceased person. Ross Gray noted in his study of bereaved teens that "frequently, the larger network of peers seemed to withdraw from the bereaved person, leaving him or her feeling socially isolated and abnormal" (Gray, 1988, p. 187).

It is rare for a teen to cry freely in front of others. Hence, grieving teens may appear to blend in with the crowd, but their attention may be focused on the inner rumblings of emotional pain.

Since adolescents have such a strong need to *identify with their peers,* connecting with a small group dealing with similar issues can be life saving. Often there is a magic that happens when they describe the mood swings, alienation, and insecurities. Some teens begin to ask, "Am I going crazy, or what?" Being with peers who also are wrestling with the craziness of grief is very comforting and keeps them coming back to the group week after week.

Some teens may choose not to share grief experiences because they feel shy or too uncomfortable. As a concerned leader, initially, you might feel that it is your responsibility to get them to talk. Experts remind us, however, that these teens can benefit vicariously from what others have to say. Learning about grief in a group setting does not need to be threatening.

The teens in the group serve as valuable **resource persons** for one another. As they tell their stories of loss and provide practical hints of how they are able to cope with various situations, they learn how to break down problems into manageable parts and receive support for trying new behaviors.

The group is a **safe place** to share a memento of a loved one, or recall a pleasant, or not-so-pleasant, memory. When tears are shed, there is not only relief but also an understanding that comes with shared pain.

Many teens are persuaded to try individual therapy with a counselor, social worker, psychologist, or even psychiatrist. Some drop out of the one-to-one experience because of the stigma of seeing a "shrink." Others feel anxious not knowing what to say, and a few admit not talking about what was really important. Most express a desire just to be understood.

Teens who have had a good experience with professionals on a one-to-one basis also can benefit from the peer support of the group. When a teen is suicidal, a leader needs to advise the parent that the services of a mental health professional are necessary in addition to meeting with the group. With the permission of the parent and the teen, the group leader could collaborate with that professional in order to better guide the teen. (More information is provided on the topic of referrals in chapter 14.)

Grieving teens can be gathered to form a group in many settings: within a particular school or within a cluster of schools, at a church or synagogue, at a hospice meeting place, or at a youth center. Individual mental health professionals and funeral home personnel often have formed such groups.

## WHAT TYPE OF GROUP?

Group guidance is an effective model for teen grief. It is *not* therapy. Rather, it is a gathering to provide support to prevent the development of more serious problems. Grief that is buried or ignored may surface later as health and emotional difficulties.

The group leaders provide some general information about grief and its effect on people's lives. They plan the topics around issues that are most important to the members. This structure helps the teens focus on painful grief-related issues.

For some groups, the flow of the discussion is spontaneous and moves easily. Other groups have difficulty bonding or have members who are reticent to share. Therefore, it is helpful to have a tentative agenda planned. There are many ideas listed within the Specific Structured Activities located in Part B to facilitate discussion.

The emphasis, however, must be on the immediate issues of the teens during that session. Whatever may be triggered in anyone in the group needs attention. Many agendas will be scratched in favor of what carries the most energy at that time. As a leader, your task is to respond to what is important to the teens in your group.

# TEEN GRIEF SUPPORT: GOAL AND OBJECTIVES

In order to stay focused in supporting grieving teens, an important procedure is to state your goal and objectives. The goal and objectives can be revised as you interact with the teen(s). Modify your approach according to the particular needs of each person. The following will assist you with the process.

## Goal

To provide a safe, supportive atmosphere for grieving teens where they can explore the effects of having a loved one die and where they can move into a better emotional balance.

## Objectives

1.  To provide accurate, appropriate information about the process of grief and how it affects one's life.
2.  To enable teens to express their fears, anger, regrets, sadness, desires, and concerns if they are willing.
3.  To help teens address various aspects of grief through specific structured activities.
4.  To assist teens in examining their current support system and learning how to expand it. This expansion may include finding an appropriate mental health professional for some teens.
5.  When in a group setting, to encourage teens to consult with other group members, as well as the leaders, as resources in exploring grief-related issues.

# USING THESE IDEAS WITH AN INDIVIDUAL TEEN

Throughout this book, great emphasis has been placed on working with bereaved teens in a group setting, principally to alleviate the isolation the grieving teen often experiences. However, there are teens who will not take the risk of joining a group of strangers or whose sports practices and extracurricular events conflict with the time when others can meet. There may not be a group situation available in some instances.

"If my teen was grieving, I could use this book to help her," fellow writer, Barbara, told me after reading a section of this manuscript. I then realized that much of this information could be adapted to use with an individual teen. How often does a school or church professional, scout leader, or mentor connect with a teen who is attempting to unravel the web of sadness after a friend or family member has died? When that moment occurs, an adult could explain the grieving process informally and engage the teen in processing his or her own grief through some of the activities in this book. The definition of "leader," used with many of the ideas in this book, could be broadened to include these adults.

If a teen senses in an adult sincerity, along with a willingness to listen without judging, that adult may help the teen explore the sources of stress and ways of creating a balance. If there is already a rapport, the teen may be open to using art, music, and writing to reflect upon personal issues and be willing to share the struggle of grappling with and moving through the anger, sadness, guilt, or any of the other emotions that can have paralyzing effects.

When appropriate, a helping adult may choose to talk about personal experiences of grief. This self-disclosure can relieve the isolation that often separates the grieving teen from others. The teen is no longer alone, struggling with the craziness of grief.

A simple comment such as, "These are difficult times" or "Would you be interested in learning some ways to handle your stress?" may open the all-important doors to understanding.

That same adult can spot the "red flag" warnings found in the section on "How to Determine When Additional Help Is Needed" (chapter 14) and help the teen obtain professional help, when needed.

There are many opportunities for caring adults to give teens, individually or in a group, permission to feel what is buried within in order to free up that energy as they journey through the healing process of grief.

# Chapter 3

# LEADERS OF A GRIEF GROUP

Needless to say, adults who will be facilitating support groups for grieving teens need to be chosen with care. A description of characteristics and skills of an effective leader is given in this chapter. The rationale for employing co-leaders also is provided.

## CHARACTERISTICS

The key to success in working with teens is to have leaders who like to work with and be with teens. These adults need to appreciate the intensity of the struggle and provide steadiness as teens wrestle with the chaos of grief. Teens are able to sense when adults are genuinely interested in their concerns.

Leaders need to provide a nonthreatening, safe atmosphere in order to earn the trust of troubled teens. Someone who is able to listen in an empathetic manner will enable teens to talk out and sort through the many problems competing for their attention.

Since the concerns of each group vary, the leaders will need to be flexible in planning and willing to allow the group to unfold. The group guidance model is different from a teaching model. Although there is some imparting of information regarding grief, a primary focus is facilitating what is most important to the teens. Leaders, therefore, need to be self-assured enough to deal with the uncertainty of tentative planning.

Finally, there are appropriate times when leaders can demonstrate that they have dealt with grief issues in their own lives and acknowledge their own personal growth from these experiences.

This self-disclosure can help clarify an abstract concept and help teens know that others actually have grown through their experiences of grief. Once again, the teens will know that they too have the opportunity to grow through the pain.

A guideline for choosing a caring person to help another who is hurting is to ask yourself two questions:

"If I were hurting, what characteristics would a person need to have in order for me to talk with that person?"
"If I had a secret, who could I tell?"

This type of person often proves to be a good choice, if he or she is able to establish a good rapport with teens.

# SKILLS

Leaders need group dynamics training to effectively promote interaction within the group and thus enable each person to speak comfortably. The art of facilitating a group effectively takes time to develop. Ideally, at least one of the leaders should have some past group experience.

Since there is a guidance component to a grief group, leaders need to transmit information that is relevant to the particular situation. Leaders need to have a good sense of timing, knowing when to teach and when to listen and support the expression of the struggle.

# WHY HAVE CO-LEADERS?

The advisable procedure is to have *two* persons leading a group. Of particular value is to have one male and one female.

When group members are exploring their grief, often many things are happening simultaneously. At these times, as well as others, having two leaders can be very valuable. One or the other leader always can be monitoring the activity level of the group.

Additionally, two persons bring different styles that can serve the group members better. Some teens may connect with one leader, while others may relate better to another leader. It is imperative, however, that the leaders be collaborative. If misunderstandings arise, it is essential that both leaders be willing and able to work out their differences *outside* the group time.

Sometimes, a bereaved teen may express something that triggers some unexpected reaction within one leader. Sensing that, the other leader may need to take over the discussion, temporarily allowing the other leader to refocus.

Practically speaking, if one leader suddenly comes down with the flu or some other emergency arises, the meeting still can be held. Unnecessary cancellations can be disruptive to the participants. The teens depend upon this all-important continuity.

Highly recommended is that one of the two leaders be a mental health professional. If this is not possible, however, it is essential that there is a professional with whom the leaders can consult. This professional can assist the leaders with group process, can assist with particular issues needing expert opinion, and can help determine when individual psychiatric help might be warranted.

# Chapter 4

# PARENTS' ROLES

This chapter highlights the results of a study on how teens perceive their parents as helping them move through the grieving process. Some of the difficulties that surface at this time are described, as well as what seems to facilitate communication between parent and teen.

Additional suggestions are given for how a leader can be an actual help to the parent. Guidelines are presented for beginning a group for parents of the attendees of the teen grief group.

## HOW CAN PARENTS BE HELPFUL TO THEIR GRIEVING TEENS?

Although 34% of grieving teens reported that their surviving parent was "helpful," 30% rated the parent as "not at all helpful." "Of those teens who found parents unhelpful, some reported wishing they had received more support, but others reported that they had been unable or unwilling to accept support that was offered" (Gray, 1988, p. 187).

### When Support Is Difficult to Accept

Those teens who were "unable or unwilling to accept support" might be demonstrating the typical communication difficulties between teens and parents. Teens simply may be obeying that inner voice so necessary to allow their own identity to emerge. For some, this involves no longer looking to a parent for support during hard times. The doors to communication may have been closed from the inside, the teen's side.

When one parent dies, some teens are apprehensive to talk to the remaining parent for fear of upsetting that parent who is now widowed. It may be too difficult to see the utter weakness of that adult on whom the teen is still somewhat dependent. It is scary enough to watch one parent die, without being constantly reminded that the other parent is so vulnerable. When it is too painful to share, some teens shut down.

## When Support Is Difficult to Give

In other cases, the parent already may have closed the communication door with the teen. The surviving parent may be so consumed by pain that there is little emotional energy to deal with the grief of the children, whatever the ages may be. Some parents may not even realize the impact the death has on the children. The children often are called "the forgotten mourners."

In some cases, the deceased parent has been the central figure in promoting communications. After that person's death, the whole family system is now out of sync. A sense of unity may have vanished. That becomes yet another loss for the family members. The remaining parent may need to develop communications skills, skills that previously were not as essential to the family functioning. This takes time and energy. It may be a very slow process. In the meantime, the teen may feel abandoned.

## When Parent and Child Can Share Their Grief

Within more resilient families, members have the coping skills for effectively solving problems and creating healthier patterns of dealing with grief. If a parent is willing to struggle with the pain of grief and talk openly about the person who has died, this openness provides a valuable bond between parent and teen.

The parent becomes a model to enable the teen to wrestle with the difficult feelings that accompany grief. Such an empathic parent is likely to see a mental health professional in order to develop the coping skills to maintain a desirable level of functioning. This ongoing support enhances the family relationships and often facilitates sharing of grief.

# HOW CAN PARENTS BE HELPED ALSO?

When there is a teen grief group in operation, it soon becomes apparent to the leaders that some of the topics are typical adolescent issues, not necessarily related to the loss of a loved one. Parent and teen communication is a challenge under the best of circumstances. With the changes in family dynamics and the intensity of the feelings while grieving, a stony silence between father and daughter or a screaming episode between mother and son is more than likely to occur.

In seeking new ways of approaching a parent, teens have expressed their feelings of inadequacy and fear of opening the doors of communication. They even have said jokingly that the parents needed the training more than they did. In reality, both parent and teen need help during the grieving process.

# PROVIDE A PARENT GROUP ALSO

It is possible to offer parent meetings during the same months that the teen groups meet. Consider scheduling them at the same time, since often parents provide transportation for their teens.

Some groups focus on any concerns the parents may have in dealing with their own grief. Just dealing with their own grief may enable some parents to better help their teens. However, other groups emphasize how parents can help their grieving teens directly. Leaders could begin by asking the parents what are their greatest concerns regarding their teens. Information could be given about teen grief as explained in chapter 1, Teens and the Grieving Process.

The leaders of the parent group could obtain information from the leaders of the teen group about what the tentatively planned topics for a given session are. Thus, the parent may be able to connect with the teen after the group if circumstances present themselves.

Confidentiality always must be maintained within the group, particularly if the leaders of the parent group are the same as the leaders of the teen group. Some teens have objected vigorously to the idea of a corresponding parent group. When the concept of a parent group was first discussed with one group of teens, one response was, "As long as *you* don't lead the group. My dad needs to learn some communications skills, but I don't want him to be able to figure out my complaints against him. Could you get other leaders?" Since we knew these teens so well, that seemed the best plan.

# Chapter 5

# PREPARATION FOR THE GROUP

Early publicity across a broad spectrum of locales where teens are serviced will help determine whether or not enough participants will register. It takes a while for the information about the group to filter through networks in order to reach the maximum number of bereaved teens.

This chapter enables leaders to see the total picture of practical tasks needing attention. A core group of interested persons could divide up the tasks, contact valuable publicity persons, and put the necessary wheels in motion. Sample copies of forms for press releases, brochures, and registration are provided. These can be modified according to specific circumstances.

In order to make teens feel welcome, an initial phone call is encouraged. Planning popular snacks is another necessary ingredient for creating a comfortable atmosphere.

## PUBLICIZING THE GROUP

### Create a Press Release

The wording of the press release is significant. The term **support group** seems threatening, according to teens. As one teen said with reservation, "When you call it a support group, it sounds like you expect us to come and spill our guts to a bunch of strangers."

Teens have suggested that we describe the group as a course on grief and list issues related to grief. Then add that the concerns of group members also will be included in the sessions.

Two sample news releases are provided in Figures 5.1 and 5.2.

### Create a Brochure

Design a handout (brochure) that captures the essence of your group. Enclose a copy with the press release to give to interested individuals.

# NEWS RELEASE 1

**Support for Bereaved Teens**

The death of a loved one often is accompanied by feelings of isolation, confusion, depression, as well as a lack of energy and declining grades. [Hospice Services] is sponsoring a 6-session series on "Issues of Grief" for teens who have experienced the death of a relative or friend.

Topics will include the following:

- Bereavement: What Is It and How Does It Feel?,

- Taking Care of Yourself,

- Dealing with Lower Grades,

- Coping with Changes, and

- Other Topics Proposed by the Participants.

This program begins [insert date, time, and place].

More information and registration forms are available at [insert phone number].

---

**Figure 5.1.**   Sample of a news release.

# NEWS RELEASE 2

**Support for Bereaved Teens**

Holiday time can trigger feelings of isolation, confusion, and depression if you have had someone close to you die. [Hospice Services] is sponsoring a 6-session series on "Issues of Grief" for teens who have experienced the death of a relative or friend. Topics will include the following:

- Bereavement: What Is It and How Does It Feel?,

- Grief and the Holidays,

- Dealing with Stress,

- Coping with Changes, and

- Other topics proposed by the participants.


This program begins [insert date, time, and place].

To obtain more information or to register, call [insert phone number].

---

**Figure 5.2.**   Sample of a news release.

A sample brochure is provided in Figure 5.3. This brochure is designed to be folded in thirds and personalized by the sponsoring organization.

## Distribute the Information

Send press releases and brochures to local hospices, school system public information offices, and church/synagogue bulletins. Post them on bulletin boards anywhere that youth may go. Newspapers and radio stations may offer public service announcements free of charge to nonprofit organizations.

Often, bulletins and newsletters require a substantial amount of lead time before including a release in their publication. This requires early planning in preparation for the group.

## Contact Key Persons

Call persons who work with youth and tell them about the group. Ask if they would talk with bereaved teens with whom they may connect and give them a brochure. Examples of key persons are the following:

hospice personnel,
church/synagogue youth directors,
school psychologists/counselors/principals/teachers,
mental health professionals,
neighborhood youth directors,
sports coaches/directors, and
former participants.

# INTERVIEW AND REGISTRATION

## Prepare a Registration Form

Decide what information is both essential and helpful for you, as leaders, to know before the group begins.

Eventually, a roster list with addresses and phone numbers may be compiled and distributed to the group members. A sample registration form is provided in Figure 5.4. (Note permission for inclusion on the roster list in Figure 5.4.)

## Send the Registration Form to Interested Teens

When a parent, guidance counselor, or other adult advocate calls about a particular teen, send a registration form to be completed by the parent or guardian.

# TEEN GRIEF GROUP—SPONSORED BY [HOSPICE SERVICES]

## Why Come to a Teen Grief Group?

- To learn about the grief: What is it? How does it feel? What helps to get through it?
- To meet other grieving teens with similar issues, regrets, concerns, adjustments.
- To learn to relax, gain energy, release bottled up feelings, and thus move toward a better balance in life.

-----Fold-----

## Who Is Invited?

- Any teen, ages 12 to 19, who has had someone close die, be it parent, grandparent, sibling, other relative, or friend.
- Any teen who is tired of feeling isolated by the pain of loss.
- Any teen who is coping with changes as a result of the death of a loved one.

-----Fold-----

## What Do We Do?

- Talk about how the feelings related to grief affect our lives and how we can work through some of the pain.
- Listen to others speak of memories about the person who died and add our own memories, if we wish.
- Talk about problem areas such as declining grades, reactions of friends, dealing with anger, moodiness, crying, and any other topic that may come up.
- Eat, drink, and socialize.

**Figure 5.3, page 1.**   Sample wording for an 8.5″ × 11″ size brochure to be folded in thirds.

**Issues Discussed in Former Groups**

- declining grades
- meddling relatives
- preparing for the holidays

- putting fun things back into my life
- expanding my support system

**How to Care for Myself While Feeling**

- sad
- angry

- lonely
- fearful

- confused
- depressed

- guilty
- frustrated

-----Fold-----

Name
Address [of sponsoring organization]

```
┌─────────────────────────────┐
│                             │
│       **Address Label**         │
│                             │
└─────────────────────────────┘
```

-----Fold-----

# TEEN GRIEF GROUP—[HOSPICE SERVICES]

"I thought my feelings were dumb and was ashamed of
them. Then I came to this group and realized that others
have the same feelings. When I am with others outside this
group, I feel abnormal. Here I feel more secure. I am a normal grieving person."

Laurie, 15, about Teen Grief Group

---

**Figure 5.3, page 2.**    Sample wording for an 8.5″ × 11″ size brochure to be folded in
thirds.

**Teen Grief Group Registration Form**

Teen's Name _____

Address _____

City, Zip _____   Phone _____

School _____   Year in school _____

Date of birth _____   Age _____

Parent(s) Name(s) _____

Work phone: Mother _____   Father _____

Sibling(s) name(s) and age(s) _____  _____  _____

_____  _____  _____

Name of person who died _____

Date of death _____

Relationship with teen _____

Cause of death _____

Have there been other significant changes in your teen's life?

_____

_____

**Figure 5.4, page 1.**   Sample registration form.

Are there other concerns for your teen on which you wish to comment?

_____

_____

Is transportation needed to or from the group? _____

May we include your teen's name, phone number, and address on the roster list that will be given to the other group members? Y_____    N _____

In case of emergency, if parent is not reachable, list someone you would like us to contact.

Name  _____    Phone _____

If your teen is seeing a mental health professional, could the leader of the group contact that person, if necessary? Y  _____    N_____

If that occasion should occur, the leader will tell you. Confidentiality will be maintained at all times.

Name of professional  _____    Phone _____

**Parent/Guardian Signature** _____    **Date** _____

**Figure 5.4, page 2.**    Sample registration form.

Send a cover letter specifying times, place, directions, names of leaders, fees, if appropriate, and any other necessary information. Ask that the form be returned a week before the first meeting to allow time for the leaders to peruse the forms and talk with the teen.

### Call the Teen before the First Meeting

After the teen has made the initial contact, personally or through an adult, one of the leaders needs to call or meet with each new teen. The leader can explain how the group runs, touch on what topics will be discussed, and offer to answer any questions about the group. The leader should explain the **rule of confidentiality** to reassure the teen.

In this meeting, the leader should have a chance to ask about the person who has died and how things are going for the teen. The leader also can assess whether or not this group is appropriate for this particular teen.

This initial phone call may alleviate the anxiety the teen may experience when anticipating being with a bunch of strangers. The teen now has connected with at least one person who will be in the group.

The leader can leave a phone number and encourage the teen to call if any questions or concerns arise.

## DON'T FORGET THE SNACKS

The highlight of any teen gathering is the food. Large bowls of popcorn being passed around the circle can help reduce tension during anxious moments. Although each group has its favorites, pizza, crackers and cheese, pretzels, soda, and hot chocolate have been the staples for many of our groups.

Sometimes a teen will volunteer to bring in a specialty, but keep it voluntary. As one leader said, "Many of them are adjusting to the loss of their mom who was also the cook." By supplying the snacks, the leaders may simplify the teen's task of getting to the meeting.

Before the arrival of the entire group, the pouring of soft drinks and gathering of the snacks becomes a meaningful ritual. It can be a time of light bantering. Since the teens may come from different schools, they can pass on information about who knows whom or make comments about rival sports teams.

When members become more comfortable, they even may offer to plan an opener for the next session. A joke or puzzle-solving session, appropriately timed, adds to the camaraderie of the group members.

This time for bonding is well spent.

# Chapter 6

# FRAMEWORK FOR THE SESSIONS

This chapter addresses practical aspects of the design of the group. Recommendations regarding length of a session, number of meetings, number of activities per session, and choosing a place are made.

A specific outline for those first two all-important meetings is presented. Some of the logistical concerns include confirming time and place and deciding upon inclement weather and transportation plans. Besides the practical concerns, the leaders are challenged with making the teens feel comfortable as they introduce themselves and begin to tell their stories. Emphasizing ground rules of respect and confidentiality can help establish that safe atmosphere.

The middle section of chapter 6 addresses the structure for meetings three through the end. Chapters 9, 10, and 11 contain a wide variety of activities dealing with different dimensions of the grieving process. This variety provides leaders with a great amount of latitude to choose what will meet the needs of their particular teens.

The final section of chapter 6 includes a rationale for preparing teens for the ending of the group. This is a good time to help teens examine their support systems to determine if they need to expand their networks. This end-of-group session lends itself to obtaining feedback about the group through an evaluation. Some practical activities to assist with closure are suggested.

## GROUP DESIGN

### Length of a Typical Session

A typical session is 75 to 90 minutes long. The ending time includes a range of up to about 15 minutes to allow a teen to finish speaking rather than cut off the sharing to have a punctual ending. This need for flexibility ought to be explained to parents who are often the drivers.

**Number of Meetings**

Although an 8-week group is ideal, often teens are only willing to commit to 6 weeks. Some teens come back for a second set of sessions, either as participants or as peer facilitators. There is some repetition; however, leaders can vary the plans enough to make it a growth-filled experience. The group may wish to continue meeting beyond the agreed upon length of time or return for a reunion group. Since this structure fosters bonding among the members, a policy would need to be determined about allowing new members to join (e.g., after the second meeting, no new members).

Some leaders prefer an ongoing drop-in group (e.g., twice a month) to better accommodate new members. Depending upon the setting, this would enable some flexibility for the attendees to work around their schedules.

**Number of Activities per Meeting**

Leaders could plan two or three activities depending upon the number of participants and their willingness to talk. It is advisable to overplan, rather than not have enough. If the teens are particularly talkative, some parts can be rescheduled for the following week. The immediate concerns of the teens take priority over a scheduled agenda.

**Choosing the Space**

An open space with comfortable chairs is an ideal setting for a teen group. However, other structures will work. Some meetings require a table with chairs allowing enough elbow room to do an art project. Some teens prefer to meet around tables continually, giving them easy access to snacks. Gathering in a circle of chairs or even on a carpet would facilitate some other activities. The outdoors on a pleasant day might be the perfect setting for the initial icebreakers or the closing affirmation activity.

Try various configurations. Gain input from the teens. Be creative in using whatever is available and molding it to the needs of your particular group.

# THE FIRST TWO MEETINGS

The first two meetings set the tone for the remaining sessions. Often, teens are nervous and avoid eye contact. While some are withdrawn, others may talk non-stop. Leaders need to be settled rather than be scurrying about with last minute preparations. The welcoming, nonjudgmental attitude of the leaders helps reduce the tension. The activity around pouring drinks and obtaining snacks provides a nonverbal connectedness and increases the comfort level of all.

**Introductions**

It may be easier for a teen to speak with one other person before addressing the whole group. Breaking up into pairs allows the teen to hear his or her own voice in a normal way.

There are icebreaker activities from which to choose in chapter 7, Helping Teens Connect.

**Confidentiality**

Rules and clear boundaries create the safety necessary for self-disclosure. Therefore, it is essential to establish the ground rule of confidentiality at the beginning of the first meeting. Self-conscious teens are cautious about sharing private information about themselves if they feel that it might be made public or be misused. If the group members agree that a personal story stays within the confines of their meeting room, teens may speak more openly about important issues.

However, it is all right to talk about general information regarding grief, or about your personal insights. For example, "Now I better understand why my grades have dropped. A lot of grieving people have a hard time concentrating." It is *not* all right to mention personal content that someone else shares. For example, "See that girl over there in the bleachers? She is in a group with me and was really upset at our last meeting. Her brother died of AIDS." Group members expect confidentiality to be kept.

The concept of confidentiality may be difficult to learn from an explanation. At various times throughout the meetings, a leader may differentiate further between what is okay and what is not okay by using examples from that particular session (e.g., "It is all right to share that a lot of grieving teens are angry at meddling relatives, overprotective parents, or incompetent doctors. It is not okay to say, 'Sylvia, who is in my teen group, ran away from home because her dad is too confining.'")

There are some gray areas. The teens themselves could be brought into the discussion of what they would expect to be kept confidential and what is all right to share. Encourage teens that when they are in doubt, they should ask one another.

**Value of Working in a Group**

Share with the teens some of the highlights from chapter 2, The Value of a Group in Dealing with Grief.

1. Grief groups can reduce feeling of isolation of bereaved teens.
2. Other teens may have ideas of how to deal with similar situations, feelings, or issues.
3. Leaders have information about the grieving process and how to move through it with some sense of balance.

## Housekeeping Information

Provide specific information about the place, time, and frequency of meetings, as well as inclement weather plans, absentee notification, and transportation issues. This will help prevent confusion later.

## Ground Rules

Discuss ground rules such as the following.

1.  Physical violence is totally unacceptable and will not be tolerated in this group setting.
2.  Each person is encouraged to speak, but no one will be coerced to do so.
3.  Each person is expected to listen to whomever is speaking and refrain from criticizing another. A member may add something, but needs to be accepting of another's sharing.

## Descriptions of Grief

**Grief** is the normal process that occurs after a person has experienced the loss of a loved one. This group focuses on loss as a result of death of a loved one. Acknowledging the pain of grief, and learning ways to deal with it, leads toward healing and growth.

The section on "The Process of Grief" in chapter 1 has some valuable information to communicate on the process of grief. More specific activities are listed in chapter 8, Learning about Grief.

## Telling Their Stories

It is important for the teens to be able to talk about the death of their loved ones in order to make the death real. There are questions in the Activity 11.1, "Telling One's Story," in chapter 11 to assist the teen in focusing on various aspects of the death. Sometimes hearing someone else talk about the loss of a loved one can make it easier to tell one's own story. A leader or peer facilitator who has experienced the death of a loved one may be encouraged to go first.

The teens could be nudged gently into telling their stories yet not be put on the spot. Remember, even if someone chooses not to speak, that person still may benefit from listening to others tell their stories. There is a certain connectedness in knowing that another person of the same age has experienced a loss, even if the details are different. This bond often can be seen in the faces of the listeners or in the nodding of the heads. There is that sense, "I am not alone."

# THE MIDDLE MEETINGS

During the first two or even three meetings, leaders will have gleaned some information about what important issues need to be addressed. This will influence the planning for the meetings that follow.

The Specific Structured Activities, Part B of this book, include many diverse practical plans to help the teens focus on issues relating to their grief. Plan one meeting at a time. What comes up spontaneously is more important to focus on than a preplanned program. A spirit of flexibility will ensure that teens will claim the group as their own and will, therefore, continue to come to meetings.

# CLOSURE: SAYING GOOD-BYE TO THE GROUP

## Importance of Closure

"Do we have to stop?" whispered a shy 13-year-old girl. "I wish this group could go on and on." Others agreed, saying that the group was very important to them in their struggle with loss, and they didn't want to lose *it*, too.

The bonds developed in a caring group are very difficult to let go of because it seems like another loss in the teen's lives. Therefore, leaders should prepare the group for closure gently, but firmly.

Plan a series of between six and eight sessions. If some teens need more time with a grief group, it may be advisable to end that series, take a month off, and begin another set of sessions. That month between groups gives leaders time to advertise the start of a new group and accept newcomers as well as former participants.

Those who wish to end then will have a chance to say good-bye. Some are ready for the group to be over. They may have completed the number of sessions agreed upon with a parent and would feel put upon if more sessions were added to this series. These reluctant attendees had fulfilled their agreement and are ready to stop.

When the new group begins, some teens who had attended a former group may wish to become peer facilitators. This enables them to assume some leadership within the group and still participate as members. These peer helpers can lead "getting to know you" exercises, making new members feel welcome, and assist with facilitating the discussions. Just by sharing first, they can enable others to follow their lead.

## Ending a Group

**Looking at the Support System.** At the next to the last session, begin talking about ending the group. The activity, "Supports in My Life," in chapter 12 helps both teens and leaders look at the extent of each person's network. If there are not enough supportive persons in a teen's daily life, the leader may help generate ideas for how to include others. For some teens, this expansion even may involve a mental health professional.

Often teens are reluctant to see a mental health professional, so the leader needs to tread cautiously. The leader could talk about the value of seeing a professional counselor temporarily, to help the teens develop the skills to move through grief in a healthy way. Just as a person with a broken leg needs to visit the doctor regularly to oversee the healing of the leg, it is not unusual for a grieving person to meet with a professional. Some group members already may have enough support persons in their lives; others may need to add some.

Information about local mental health resources, and particularly the phone number of a crisis hotline, should be made available to the teens.

**Saying Good-bye to the Group Members.** There is often pain in the good-bye, yet acknowledging that pain enables people to move on. During the last session, allow time for group members to evaluate what was helpful and not so helpful in the group sessions. Then allow time for teens to say what they will miss and what they will take with them from this grief group. There are a variety of appropriate activities described in chapter 12, Completing the Group Experience.

Some groups are comfortable with a simple ending; others may prefer a picnic, ice cream party, or gathering at a restaurant on the last day.

If a roster of names and phone numbers has not been distributed previously, this would be a good opportunity to have copies of the roster available. Close bonds may have formed in the group, and the roster may be the avenue to nurture these relationships.

## Obtaining Feedback from Participants

Evaluating the group's activities reinforces the reality that the group is ending and provides helpful information for the leaders as they plan for future groups. More information about evaluation, along with samples, can be found in chapter 13, Evaluation.

# PART B
# SPECIFIC STRUCTURED ACTIVITIES

*Ideally,* the teens will gather and begin to share the pain of their own stories of grief. Gradually, they learn to listen attentively to the tales of the others in the group, offer an encouraging word, or share a similar insight. Although this sometimes occurs, it is not the norm.

In *reality,* the chemistry of the group depends upon who comes. Sometimes the leaders can hardly get a word in. One time, the issue being discussed was feeling awkward about crying in public, and everyone could relate to it. Another meeting centered on one teen's comment about some relative who had called him "the man of the family" now that his dad had died. There was a bond, a magical connection within the group.

At other times, the teens seem worlds apart. The age range may be too great, or many are withdrawn or do not want to be there. The silence may be deafening. The anxiety level may increase, adding one more pressure.

At such times, leaders might have to pull together ideas and develop a structure to help the teens focus upon some aspect of grief. The group could determine what issues are pertinent for them, and then the leaders could have something available to facilitate the discussion.

The group's goal is to engage the teens in the process of grief. If they are able to move with their own issues naturally, fewer structured activities are used. Their own spontaneous discussion of issues related to grief always takes priority. The agenda prepared by the leaders is secondary to the immediate needs of the day.

There may be participants who seldom speak during the sessions, even when a structured activity is used. Experts assure us that even the silent members of the group can benefit from being there and listening to the others.

As leaders, you may decide to use part of one activity and connect it with an idea of your own or with something that evolves in the group. Someone may want to share a newly written poem, or one that he or she just discovered. A magazine article, drawing, or song may resonate with the experiences of your specific group.

# Chapter 7

# HELPING TEENS CONNECT

A very worthwhile procedure during the first two or three meetings is to spend 20 or 30 minutes on fun activities that will help the teens get to know one another, as well as lessen the anxiety that often accompanies the beginning of a group. These nonintrusive icebreakers foster trust among the participants, which is invaluable in enabling them to share their very personal experiences of the many facets of grief during later sessions.

# Activity 7.1. GETTING TO KNOW YOU

## Goal

To help teens connect with other group members.

## Objectives

1. To get to know something about other group members.

2. To remember to do enjoyable things, even while grieving.

## Introductory Comments

These are a few ideas to lighten the atmosphere as teens who do not know one another come together. The leaders may choose from their own repertoire of icebreakers, such as the suggested activities that follow.

## Procedure

1. Ask teens to fold a sheet of paper into eight parts, move around the room, and ask each person to sign one of the blocks and write down on that block something that he or she likes to do. (15 minutes)

2. Form a circle. Throw a bean bag, a light beach ball, or a small pillow around the circle. As each person catches it, have each person say his or her name. Continue with any of the ideas from the following list. Add your own. (25 to 30 minutes)

    School
    Grade
    Favorite activity
    Favorite holiday
    Favorite food
    Favorite music group
    Favorite color
    If I won $100, I would . . .
    If I won $1,000, I would . . .
    If I could travel anywhere, I would go to . . . with . . .

## Activity 7.2. MY COAT OF ARMS

**Goal**

To introduce the group members to each another.

**Objectives**

1. To assist the teens in sharing information about themselves with the group.

2. To solicit information for the leaders to plan the agenda for future sessions.

**Procedure**

1. Make 8.5″ × 11″ copies of the instructions and the blank shield (Activity Sheet 7.2) and distribute to each person to complete.

2. Have the teens choose a partner and talk about their coat of arms.

3. Return to the group. The partner then introduces the person to the group by telling about the other person's symbols. Continue until everyone is introduced.

4. If the symbols elicit further discussion, go with it. (30 to 40 minutes)

## MY COAT OF ARMS

### Draw:

1. Symbol of one thing you like to do.
2. Symbol representing a goal you accomplished in the last 3 years.
3. Symbol that reminds you of the person who died.
4. Symbol representing the worst thing about grief.
5. Words or symbol. What made you come to the group?
6. Symbol of one change you have experienced since your loved one died.

---

**Activity Sheet 7.2.**    Coat of Arms. Permission is given to photocopy for grief group use.

## Activity 7.3. QUESTIONS FOR TEENS

**Goal**

To help teens connect with group members.

**Objective**

1.   To get to know the others in the group through an interview.

**Procedure**

1.   Make a copy of "The Interview Sheet" (Activity Sheet 7.3) for each teen and each leader in the group.
2.   Distribute.
3.   Ask teens to choose someone in the room whom they do not know well.
4.   Have individuals follow directions on the "The Interview Sheet" (Activity Sheet 7.3). (20 minutes)

**The Interview Sheet**

**Directions:** Pretend you are a reporter.

a   Ask your partner the questions below.

b   When finished, have your partner ask you the same questions.

c   When called back together as a group, you will introduce your partner to the group.

1. Identifying information:

    NAME

    AGE

    SCHOOL

    GRADE

2. What is your favorite TV show?

3. What do you like to eat the best?

4. Do you have a favorite sport or physical activity?
       If yes, what is it?

5. If someone gave you $50, what would you buy?

6. If you won the million dollar lottery, what would you do?

---

**Activity Sheet 7.3.**    The Interview Sheet. Permission is given to photocopy for grief group use.

# Activty 7.4. MIRRORING

**Goal**

To connect with other group members.

**Objectives**

1. To connect in a fun way with another group member.

2. To experience various feelings and be able to name them.

**Procedure**

1. Recall with the teens that many children have played "Simon Says" and "Copycat" games over the years.

2. Help the teens realize that this activity is adapted from those games and will help them identify the variety of feelings connected with grieving.

3. Ask them to recognize, but not be surprised, when these feelings arise.

4. Have them notice the varying degree of intensity (e.g., very angry vs. annoyed).

5. Have each person choose a partner whom they do not know well.

6. Ask one person from each pair to pantomime the expression of a feeling of grief (e.g., anger, guilt, sadness, helplessness).

7. Have the partner copy the movement.

8. Then have everyone try out the feeling movement.

9. Pairs can continue to mirror various feelings. (10 minutes)

10. Discuss what can help us deal with difficult feelings. (Specific ideas are provided in chapter 10, Grappling with and Moving through the Pain.)

# Chapter 8

# LEARNING ABOUT GRIEF

The information presented about grief during the first two group sessions supports the bonding of group members. Each person has experienced the loss of a loved one. Although each grief experience is unique, often common threads draw grieving people together emotionally.

The activities in this chapter enable teens to reflect upon the grief process and gain some insight into their own experiences of grief.

Activity 8.1, "Helps in Moving through Your Grief," could take as long as one hour. It may be separated into two sessions, or the leaders may pick and choose those parts that they deem most appropriate. Activity 8.2, "Choosing to Work through Your Grief," attempts to motivate teens to do the necessary griefwork in order to feel better. If this activity is utilized, it ought to be presented on a day other than "Helps in Moving through Your Grief." "Choosing to Work through Your Grief" takes about 30 minutes.

# Activity 8.1. HELPS IN MOVING THROUGH YOUR GRIEF

## Goal

To provide information about the process of grief and an opportunity to reflect upon one's own experience of grief.

## Objectives

1. To introduce the tasks of grieving as presented by William Worden (1991).

2. To help teens identify experiences as they connect with Worden's model of grief.

3. To suggest ways of continuing the movement through grief.

## Introductory Comments

William Worden has provided a model to explain how persons accomplish particular tasks as they move through the difficult times and begin to feel more balanced. These are called the **tasks of grieving.**

- **To Accept the Reality of the Loss**—knowing the deceased person is no longer alive and will not physically be a part of their everyday lives.

- **To Experience the Pain of Grief**—experiencing a variety of intense feelings and working them through as a part of the grieving process.

- **To Adjust to an Environment in Which the Deceased Is Missing**—struggling with the many changes as a result of the death, including the practical aspects of daily living and the effects upon the sense of self and perception of the world.

- **To Emotionally Relocate the Deceased and Move on with Life**—acknowledging the value of the relationship with the deceased, yet allowing oneself to get on with life (Worden, 1991, pp. 10, 13, 14, & 16).

To understand better the **tasks of grieving,** these activities help teens connect these concepts with their own experiences. The questions are structured to enable leaders and group members to come up with other appropriate ways to move through these various tasks.

## Procedure

1. Present an explanation of the tasks of grief by William Worden to the whole group. (20 minutes)

2. Provide a large sheet of roll-out paper and some markers. Each person could write about or draw a symbol of what helps him or her with the feelings of grief. (30 minutes)

3. Construct on large paper a graphic representation of the feelings that grieving persons experience and ask the teens to identify when they experienced particular feelings. They could be encouraged to add others not represented. (Information about the Grief Art Project, which graphically illustrates the feelings of grieving, is listed under "Additional Resources" in the Resource Material section at the back of this book.) (30 minutes)

4. Make copies of Activity Sheet 8.1 and distribute them to the group. Provide time for teens to share their responses. (Because so much information is being presented, this activity could be split between two sessions. Introduce the first and second tasks one week, and the third and fourth tasks the next. (40 minutes)

## Helps in Moving through Your Grief

William Worden worked with grieving persons. He observed what they experienced as they moved through the turmoil of their grief toward a place of healing. These experiences are called the **tasks of grief.**

- **To Accept the Reality of the Loss**—knowing the deceased person is no longer alive and will not be a part of their everyday lives.

- **To Experience the Pain of Grief**—experiencing a variety of intense feelings and working them through as a part of the grieving process.

- **To Adjust to an Environment in Which the Deceased Is Missing**—struggling with the many changes as a result of the death, including the practical aspects of daily living and the effects upon the sense of self and perception of the world.

- **To Emotionally Relocate the Deceased and Move on with Life**—acknowledging the value of the relationship with the deceased, yet allowing oneself to get on with life (Worden, 1991, pp. 10, 13, 14, & 16).

### Helps in Moving through Your Grief, Part A

1. In dealing with the first task of grief, **To Accept the Reality of the Loss,** it is difficult to totally comprehend the reality of death right away. Did you find yourself:

listening for the footsteps of the person?
expecting the person to call?
hoping that there was some mistake and the person was still alive?

Jot down any similar experiences you have had.

It is painful to face the fact that the person will not return physically. However, by gently reminding yourself of the loss, it eventually will become more real.

---

**Activity Sheet 8.1, page 1.**   Helps in Moving through Your Grief, Part A. Permission is granted to photocopy for grief group use. **Source:** Adapted from *Grief Counseling and Grief Therapy, Second Edition,* by J. W. Worden. Copyright © 1991 by Springer Publishing Company, New York 10012. Used by permission.

2. In dealing with the second task of grief, **To Experience the Pain of Grief,** "I must be losing my mind," is a common complaint of the grieving person. "The least little thing really ticks me off. I yell and scream at everyone. My friends are afraid of me. I even scare myself."

Which feelings have you experienced most intensely in your grief?

anger

sadness

depression

hopelessness

guilt

loneliness

helplessness

frustration

Learn to stay with your feelings in a caring way. Be a friend to yourself by listening to your pain. Then talk with someone who listens well or make an entry in your journal (such as a poem, a drawing, a paint splash) or play some music that matches how you feel. What else helps you feel the emotion, and move through it?

---

**Activity Sheet 8.1, page 2.**   Helps in Moving through Your Grief, Part A. Permission is granted to photocopy for grief group use. **Source:** Adapted from *Grief Counseling and Grief Therapy, Second Edition,* by J. W. Worden. Copyright © 1991 by Springer Publishing Company, New York 10012. Used by permission.

**Helps in Moving through Your Grief, Part B**

3. In dealing with the third task of grief, **To Adjust to an Environment in Which the Deceased Is Missing,** the person who died may have done various jobs in the family that now must be done by someone else.

List some things that person did:

Write the names of the persons who now do those tasks:

The person who died may have been special in other ways. List special traits of that person:

List the names of others who have those traits:

---

**Activity Sheet 8.1, page 3.**    Helps in Moving through Your Grief, Part B. Permission is granted to photocopy for grief group use. **Source:** Adapted from *Grief Counseling and Grief Therapy, Second Edition,* by J. W. Worden. Copyright © 1991 by Springer Publishing Company, New York 10012. Used by permission.

4. In dealing with the fourth task of grief, **To Emotionally Relocate the Deceased and Move on with Life,** spiritual or cultural services help us remember the richness of a person's life. Often they take place shortly after the person has died; sometimes, on the anniversary of the death. In what ways has your family commemorated your loved one's life?

Allow yourself to recall the memories, both positive and negative, of the person who has died. Looking at pictures and telling stories can enrich your life and help you move through grief. List ways you can connect with your loved one.

It is okay to move on. As you move through the painful feelings, life begins to take on a new meaning. List the fun times you have had during the past month. What are some events that show that you are participating in life?

**Activity Sheet 8.1, page 4.**   Helps in Moving through Your Grief, Part B. Permission is granted to photocopy for grief group use. **Source:** Adapted from *Grief Counseling and Grief Therapy, Second Edition,* by J. W. Worden. Copyright © 1991 by Springer Publishing Company, New York 10012. Used by permission.

# Activity 8.2. CHOOSING TO WORK THROUGH YOUR GRIEF

## Goal

To promote active involvement in the grieving process, by comparing grief to other challenging activities familiar to teens.

## Objectives

1. To elicit desired goals from the teens and how they would accomplish them.

2. To enable the teens to see the correlation between working toward a goal and doing their "griefwork," to engage them in moving through grief.

## Procedure

1. Make copies of Activity Sheet 8.2, "The Work of Grief."

2. Have teens complete and share responses.

## The Work of Grief

**Grief does not just "go away."** If a person wishes to experience the fullness of living again, it is necessary to engage in the "work of grief" to eventually reach a new state of equilibrium.

1. Think of something you or someone else would like to accomplish (e.g., swim at the Olympics, play soccer on a traveling team, play the piano or the drums, learn Spanish for your vacation in Mexico). Write what you would like to accomplish.

2. List what it would take to accomplish this goal.

　　How much time would be needed for practice?

　　Who would be involved?

　　What are the expenses?

3. Share what you have written with the group.

　　**Griefwork** requires:

- **time** to think about the person who has died and what is happening in your life,

- **commitment** to learn about the grieving process and how it affects your life, and

- **willingness** to explore the pain of intense emotions and experience the relief of working them through.

---

**Activity Sheet 8.2, page 1.**　The Work of Grief. Permission is granted to photocopy for grief group use.

**You are not alone.** You have the support of these persons:

- leaders of the grief group;

- other professionals—doctors, guidance counselors, clergy/rabbis;

- other persons in the group who also are grieving; and

- a friend or family member to listen, without judging.

4. List the names of anyone who could help you with your grief.

---

**Activity Sheet 8.2, page 2.** The Work of Grief. Permission is granted to photocopy for grief group use.

# Chapter 9

# CREATING A BALANCE

Grief can cause a disequilibrium in even the most stable teen. When least expected, a word, a cereal box, a TV ad, a song, can trigger a memory of a loved one who has died.

Activities 9.1 through 9.6 in this chapter offer some practical ways of encouraging grieving persons to take care of themselves to offset the disruption of grief to their daily lives.

Almost any grief group would profit from an emphasis on self-care. If many group members are having difficulty functioning in every day living, however, leaders are encouraged to choose many activities from this chapter. The approximate time allowances are specified within each activity.

# Activity 9.1. ACHIEVING A BALANCE

## Goal

To help grieving teens achieve a better emotional balance to offset the distress of working through intense feelings.

## Objectives

1. To help teens recall those activities that they enjoyed in the past and encourage them to add those activities back into their schedules.

2. To encourage teens to consider other activities that they might like to try and take steps to begin them.

## Introductory Comments

> Grief can make you crazy. Every emotion is let loose and comes flooding in, eroding any sense of balance. The normal routine of the most stable individual can be disrupted by bursting into tears or being totally distracted by the pain of loss. There is no shortcut to make the turmoil disappear. (Perschy, 1989, p. 3)

This quotation, from an article on teen grief, describes what grief can be like. When grief consumes our lives, we often forget to take care of ourselves properly.

## Procedure

1. Distribute copies of the Activity Sheet 9.1, "Achieving a Balance," to the teens and leaders.

2. Have each person fill in the sheet.

3. Discuss.

4. Encourage the teens to provide some structure for themselves, particularly during vacation time. This exercise may be particularly helpful before winter or spring break, or as the school year ends. (20 to 30 minutes)

**Achieving a Balance**

**Introductory Comments**

Sometimes we forget to do enjoyable things while we are grieving. We just allow ourselves to become stuck in boredom. However, we can take control of the limited energy we may have and make some choices that will help ourselves feel better. This activity will help you plan to do things that you have enjoyed before your loss and encourage you to try some new things.

1. List 7 things you have enjoyed doing in the past but have not done in a while. (Do not include activities that have negative side effects, such as taking drugs, using alcohol, etc.):

<u>**Activity**</u>                                             <u>**Day**</u>

2. Draw a circle around those that you would be interested in doing again.

3. Beside each activity that you listed, write the day that you could schedule to do that activity again. If the activity involves another person, write the day you will ask that person to join you.

4. Think of activities you might like to try. What steps do you need to take to begin? Write the day you will take the first step to begin this new activity. (If you finish before the rest of the group, on the back of this sheet of paper draw yourself doing one of these fun activities.)

<u>**Activity**</u>                                             <u>**Day**</u>

5. Share your responses with the group.

---

**Activity Sheet 9.1.**    Achieving a Balance. Permission is granted to photocopy for grief group use.

## Activity 9.2. CLEARING A SPACE

### Goal

To create a peaceful space, temporarily freeing the grieving teen from some of the pressure of difficult issues and feelings.

### Objectives

1. To assist teens in naming some of the issues and feelings that are causing them difficulty.

2. To teach a process that puts parentheses around these concerns, to provide some temporary relief.

### Introductory Comments

This exercise is not for every group. The teens need to be comfortable with silence, and they need to have a certain maturity to be able to enter into the imagery.

Ask the group to reflect upon the following Chinese proverb:

> "You cannot prevent the birds of sorrow
> from flying over your head,
> but you can prevent them
> from building nests in your hair."

Sometimes we may feel like the birds have landed on our heads and are beginning the construction of a nest or two. Grieving persons need a break from the sorrow.

### Procedure

The leader can read the proverb, have the group members discuss its meaning, and then slowly guide the group through this exercise:

1.  Close your eyes. Listen to your body. Allow your imagination to move around inside, and notice where you feel tight or uncomfortable.

2.  Ask yourself, "Is there anything in my life right now that is keeping me from feeling really good?" If anything comes, put your hand on your knee so I know when to continue.

3.  See if you can set that whole thing aside, by putting it on an imaginary shelf, in a box, behind a tree, or any image that moves it away from you. If it resists, tell it that you need some space, just for now. When you have moved it away, put your hand on your knee to let me know you are finished. While you are waiting for the next step, enjoy the space you have created for yourself.

4.  Ask yourself, is there anything else keeping me from feeling really free?

5.  (Leader may repeat procedures 2, 3, and 4 a few times.)

6.  Spend some time enjoying the space you have created. It may not be totally stress-free; however, there may be some relief.

7.  Before you open your eyes, remind yourself that you can create a space for yourself. (**Source:** Adapted from *The Focusing Steps*, pp. 7–8, Copyright © 1991 by Edwin M. McMahon & Peter A. Campbell. Published by Sheed & Ward Publishing.)

**Discussion**

1. Allow time to talk about the experience. Some participants may be comfortable with it; others may not. Not every technique is helpful to everyone.

2. Remind the participants that they can return at another time to one or more of the issues or feelings they had put away. Right now, they can just enjoy the space that they have created.

3. Ask the teens about times when it would be helpful to use this exercise. (30 minutes)

# Activity 9.3. THE PRESENT

## Goal

To provide a summary sheet to assist teens in coping with their grief.

## Objectives

1. To encourage the appropriate expression of intense feelings.

2. To remind teens of activities to achieve a balance in their lives.

3. To boost self-esteem by reminding teens that they can set goals and meet them.

4. To provide a list of support resources in time of need.

## Procedure

1. Distribute copies of Activity Sheet 9.3, "The Present."

2. Ask the teens to complete the first section.

3. After the first section is complete, talk about it in the group.

4. Have the teens complete the second section.

5. Repeat procedures 2 through 4 until all four sections are complete

6. Encourage the teens to post this in a significant place at home to remind them to take care of themselves while they are doing their griefwork. (30 minutes)

Some of my favorite pastimes are:

I could try:

When I am angry, sad, depressed or frustrated, it helps me to:

I could also try:

I am proud of:

I can set a goal and meet it.

When I need to talk, these people are helpful:

If I need to talk, I could also contact:

CRISIS HOTLINE:
OTHER ADULTS:

**Activity Sheet 9.3.** The Present. Permission is granted to photocopy for grief group use.

# Activity 9.4. THE HOT-AIR BALLOON

## Goal

To assist the teens in exploring the causes of stress in their lives in order to move to a more balanced state.

## Objectives

1. To identify sources of stress and record them on the paper.

2. To examine the sources of stress, and decide what can be changed and what cannot be changed.

3. To decide what changes to make, while consulting with a partner.

## Introductory Comments

Floating through the air in a hot-air balloon is an exciting sport. People stay in a basket attached to a bag filled with warm air, just to enjoy the view or to actually race.

This hot-air balloon has bags, filled with sand, hanging from the basket to help steady the balloon. However, when the balloon begins to sag, the pilot needs to let out some of the sand in order for the balloon to rise.

These sandbags resemble stress in our lives. Some stress is fine and even necessary. When we have too much stress, however, we feel weighted down or fragmented and do not function well. This activity will help us look at the causes of the stress and decide what to change, or let go of, in order to feel more balanced.

## Procedure

1. Distribute a copy of Activity Sheet 9.4, the "Hot-Air Balloon," to each teen.

2. Ask each teen to write in each sandbag some source of stress in his or her life.

3. Ask the teens to draw a circle around those bags that they have little or no control over changing.

4. Ask the teens to draw a square around those bags that they can change in some way to make them lighter. If the problem seems overwhelming, ask them to break it down into smaller parts. Ask them to be specific about any changes they could make. Sometimes people forget how much power they really have to make simple changes.

5. Ask the teens to break into pairs. The partners can serve as consultants and further help each other look at new ways of doing things.

6. Ask them to share whatever part of their pictures they wish with the other group members.

7. If it is appropriate, close with the "Serenity Prayer."

<u>Serenity Prayer</u>

Higher Spirit,

Grant me the **serenity** to accept the things I cannot change,
The **courage** to change the things I can,
And the **wisdom** to know the difference.

(30 minutes)

**Activity Sheet 9.4.**    The Hot-Air Balloon. Permission is granted to photocopy for grief group use.

# Activity 9.5. HOW MY LIFE HAS CHANGED

**Goal**

To help teens explore the difficult aspects of change resulting from loss.

**Objectives**

1. To help teens identify some changes they have experienced since their loved one died.

2. To encourage teens to name the feelings connected with the changes and explore new ways of dealing with them.

**Introductory Comments**

When someone dies, people speak of a sense of loss. "I miss him. Life isn't the same anymore." Besides the sadness, loneliness, and turmoil, often practical changes take place. Who will fulfill those tasks the deceased person used to perform? How has our financial situation changed? Sometimes these changes are subtle, and the survivors are not even aware of the impact that these changes are having on the family members.

**Procedure**

Introduce the statement, "The **death** of a loved one results in **loss** and **change.**" This activity may be helpful in exploring this concept with the teens.

1. Ask the teens, "How are things different in your life since your loved one has died?" List the following categories on a chalkboard or on large paper. As the teens identify changes, add them next to the appropriate category (10 minutes):

- family
- friends
- activities
- school

2. Have teens choose partners and respond to the following (10 minutes):

- What I miss the most is . . .
- The changes that bother me the most are . . .

Give the teens, who wish, an opportunity to share in the group.

3. Have the teens fold a paper in half. Say, "Draw a picture of your family around the table before your loved one died. On the other half, draw a picture of your family today." Ask teens to reflect on the following (20 to 30 minutes):

- The similarities in the two pictures are . . .
- The differences in the two pictures are . . .
- What I miss the most is . . .
- The changes that bother me the most are . . .

Allow time to share with a partner or with the group.

# Activity 9.6. TWO ASPECTS OF GRIEF

**Goal**

To acknowledge the positive as well as the difficult aspects of grief.

**Objectives**

1. To acquaint teens with the Chinese characters for the word "crisis," acknowledging both the pain and the opportunities involved.

2. To enable teens to reflect upon the difficult as well as the positive aspects of grief in their own lives.

**Introductory Comments**

Most people are familiar with the difficult part of a crisis situation. Yet there are often hidden positive aspects to it as well, although we may not recognize them readily. The Chinese word "crisis" is written using two characters: one means *danger;* the other means *opportunity.*

　　Most of the emphasis in on the "danger" or the pain of grief. "Look for the Silver Lining" may sound trite and even offensive when you are grieving. However, when you have passed through some of the intense pain, you may discover some strengths or a new appreciation for life that you didn't know existed within you. This phenomenon is known as serendipity. (The dictionary defines **serendipity** as the faculty of finding agreeable things not sought for.) For instance, you may have heard about a person without use of his hands who paints beautiful landscapes using his mouth to hold the paintbrush or a blind person who has developed an acute sense of hearing.

　　People expect grief to be painful; however, research studies of grieving persons show some positive gains as well.

　　One study, entitled "Positive Outcomes of Adolescents' Experiences with Grief," involved 93 teens (Oltjenbruns, 1991). The teens were able to identify areas of growth throughout their grief processes.

　　To help the teens in your group explore the positive dimension of grief, make copies of the Activity Sheet 9.6, "Two Aspects of Grief."

## Two Aspects of Grief

The pain of grief often disturbs our equilibrium and makes us feel like we are in a crisis situation. The Chinese write the word "crisis" with two characters: one means *danger;* the other, *opportunity.*

1. Danger

When we are in danger, our emotions become very intense. Often the grieving person feels this same intensity. If we ignore the feelings, they often build up, and we feel like we are ready to explode. The slightest thing can cause the "volcano" to erupt.

What helps you deal with the intense emotions? _____

Listen to others in the group. List other suggestions for dealing with difficult feelings.

_____

_____

In discussing grief, the *danger* or painful part cannot be ignored for long and therefore gets our attention. However, grief also can provide some *opportunities.*

2. Opportunity

We each have heard of someone who encounters some adversity yet moves beyond it to do great things. We hear about people with no arms who paint beautiful pictures with a paintbrush between their teeth. Some grieving persons talk about living each day to the fullest, knowing that life is often short and unpredictable.

Many grieving teens have found that there are *positive aspects* to grief. These benefits may be subtle, like becoming more independent, learning new skills, or appreciating relationships.

List any positive aspects of grief you have experienced. _____

_____

_____

Share your list with the group.

While you are waiting for the rest of the teens to finish, draw a symbol of aspects of your grief on the back of this sheet.

---

**Activity Sheet 9.6.**   Two Aspects of Grief. Permission is granted to photocopy for grief group use.

# Chapter 10

# GRAPPLING WITH AND MOVING THROUGH THE PAIN

Just as the previous chapter offers opportunities to bring about a better balance, this chapter enables and encourages teens to enter into the pain of the feeling in order to move through it. Experts in the field of grief remind us that it is not enough to go "around" grief; the operative word is "through." An important part of the grieving process is to feel the pain, not in a masochistic way, but rather to allow the healing to take place.

Activities 10.1 and 10.2 are planned around articles that tell the stories of grieving teens. The reflection questions help the teens touch into their own stories. These articles often appeal to the more verbal teens.

Activities 10.3, 10.4, and 10.5 include practical ways of touching into the intense emotions of grief. Leaders are encouraged to be vigilant during the first two meetings so that they may be able to identify the more prevalent emotions. If it is not so apparent, the group could brainstorm feelings, and each person could name those feelings affecting him or her the most. This will give the leaders information on how to direct these activities.

When words are not enough to touch into the pain of grief, the arts offer vehicles that allow emotions to surface. Activities 10.6, 10.7, 10.8, and 10.9 offer numerous hands-on suggestions that have enabled many teens to identify, feel, and express these emotions in a safe, yet therapeutic way. The multiple approaches of writing, listening to music, painting, and/or manipulating clay not only allow for the expression of feelings, but they serve as additional sources for icebreakers to help the group members connect.

The wide variety of approaches for tapping into and moving through the pain will be helpful for even the most diverse group.

# Activity 10.1. NO WHERE TO RUN

**Goal**

To help teens recall their ways of dealing with feelings.

**Objective**

1. To use an article as a catalyst to discuss the difficulties in social situations once a loved one has died.

**Procedure**

1. Distribute copies of "No Where to Run" (Williams, 1992) (Activity Sheet 10.1.), taken from the October, 1992, issue of *Bereavement Magazine*, about the plight of Sean, a teen whose mother died during the summer. Sean's story begins with his return to school the first day in the fall and his utter frustration as he meets friends and teachers. Many grieving teens have expressed that same desire to just *run*. Have the teens read the article quietly or take turns reading it aloud. (10 minutes)

2. Ask the group, "Which of the following quotations or statements resonates with your own experience?" (10 minutes)

> "They're all laughing and talking about what a great time they had this summer. I wish I could do the same. I spent my summer in hospitals and finally in a funeral home, grieving." (Sean thinking)
> Sean didn't want to be different, but it was impossible to be the same.
> "I heard about your loss, and I'm sorry. I know you're not a sissy or anything like that. I'm counting on you. Don't mess things up for us this season, Sean. Be tough." (Coach's words)
> At family functions, no one even mentioned Sean's mom. It was difficult for him to grasp why everyone considered her death such a taboo subject. It made him so mad!
> "Aren't you over that yet? It's been a couple of months already. Get on with your life, Buddy Boy." (Joe's [Sean's friend] words)
> "If nobody close to me will talk to me about it, who can I turn to? There has to be somebody who can help me. I feel like I am going insane. I honestly don't think anyone understands my problem. I think I am about to E-X-P-L-O-D-E! Somebody please help me!" (Sean's thinking)

3. Encourage the teens to talk of their experiences meeting people after their loved one died and how they felt. (10 minutes)

4. Ask the teens what they wish people would say to them or do for them. Encourage them to consider who they could talk to when they feel like they are ready to explode. (Remind them of a hotline phone number.) (10 minutes)

5. Consider extending the discussion to continue the following week.  As they prepare to leave, encourage the teens to write, draw, or talk about how they feel during the week.

## No Where to Run

by Katie Williams, age 18

The ringing of the alarm clock jolted him from his sleep. "That damn alarm clock!" It can't be 6:30 yet; I'm not ready to go back to school. The past two weeks have been terrible; how will I ever be able to face everyone? Does everyone know my mom died? I wonder what their reactions will be.

Who is going to make my lunch? Certainly not my dad, but I wouldn't want Aunt Emily to come over and make it. It just wouldn't be the same.

Sean knew it would be impossible to concentrate on school, but he got up anyway and confronted his dad.

"Bye, Sean, have a good day!"

"Bye, Dad, I'll certainly try. You have a good day too!"

Sean thought it would have been nice if his dad had given him some reassuring words to calm his nerves a bit before he started off to school.

As soon as he arrived at school, it was time to find his locker. "Hey, look," he thought. "There are the guys: Mark, Dan and Joe. They're all laughing and talking about what a great time they had this summer. I wish I could be the same. I spent my summer in hospitals and finally in a funeral home, grieving."

"Look who's coming down the hallway, guys; it's Sean!" said Mark, then he suddenly added, "Shut up and stop laughing."

"Hi everybody, what's up?" Sean called to his friends, but he heard people whispering to each other to be quiet. As he approached, total silence fell. Sean didn't understand what was going on, why things between him and his friends were suddenly so different.

Casually, Dan announced, "My mom is so dumb! Does she really think I am still going to want peanut butter and jelly on Wonder Bread with the crusts cut off and a box drink? Does she think I'm seven years old?"

It made Sean wish he had a mom to make lunch for him. He was sure he would appreciate her, instead of criticizing a nice gesture on her part.

His first class was Spanish where they talked about their summer vacations. Sean froze when it was his turn. He couldn't just blurt out that his mom died, though that's what he really would have liked to do. He thought he would scream if each class was going to ask about his vacation.

As he walked down the hallway when Spanish class was over, a girl stopped him and said, "I heard about what happened, and I'm sorry." That is all she said on that subject, then she just continued to carry on a conversation as if nothing had happened.

It seemed to Sean that was what most of his friends were doing. They simply ignored the fact that he couldn't be like them. "I'm really not the same at all, I don't have a family anymore. Well, I don't think you could call just Dad, 'family.'"

He really wanted to get on with things and put his pain out of his mind, and on the outside he did that. But he soon decided that was a mistake. He may have looked fine; just like the same old Sean as before, laughing, making jokes and so on, but it was different now. He didn't want to be different, but it was impossible to be the same.

After lunch he proceeded to his math class. Mr. Peabody called out the role and when he got to Sean, he paused and looked up saying, "So sorry about your loss." It was nice that he acknowledged the fact that Sean's mom had passed away, but it seemed so unemotional, cold and brief. Sean felt he could have said it in a different way.

Finally it was 3:15 p.m. and Sean had made it through the first day of his return to school. "At last," he thought, "now I can go have fun at football practice."

"Hi, Coach Arnold, sure glad to be back in the swing of things. What is our practice going to be like today?"

"Oh, Sean, can you come here a minute? Listen, I heard about your loss, and I'm sorry, but don't think that is going to make any changes occur on this team. I still expect you out there playing fullback, giving the game one hundred percent, you hear? I know you're not a sissy or anything like that. Well, you better not be 'cause I'm counting on you. Don't mess things up for us this season, Sean. Be tough."

What could he possibly say after a speech like that? He just buried his feelings again.

As time passed, Sean continued to face the same indifferent reactions from teachers, friends, coaches and even his dad, whom he had expected to be there for him. His dad never liked discussing his feelings about Sean's mom's death and that only made Sean feel like he couldn't say anything, either. The only person Sean felt he could relate to was his Uncle Larry, but he lived in Arizona, so that wasn't much help.

Sean felt so lost, as if there were no one he could turn to. At family functions, no one even mentioned his mom. It was difficult for him to grasp why everyone considered her death such a taboo subject. It made him so mad! "Doesn't anyone care about how I'm feeling?" Sean wondered. "It certainly doesn't seem that way."

"Sean, why do you seem so down? Girl trouble again?" asked Joe. Sean wondered why people automatically attributed his being upset to girl trouble.

"No, Joe, it's a bit more complicated than that."

"What could possibly be wrong? At least you don't have parents that are always ordering you around. What . . . why are you looking at me like that?"

"That's just it, Joe, I don't have parents. I have A PARENT."

"Aren't you over that yet? It's been a couple of months already. Get on with your life, Buddy Boy. You can't just sit there sulking for the rest of your life."

Sean stood, speechless thinking to himself, "Nobody realizes the pain I am going through. My dad must be experiencing similar things, he will know what to say to me."

Sean's dad picked him up after football practice, and Sean thought this was his chance. With nothing to distract them, his dad would have to listen to him now. "Dad, I have been having the roughest time at school."

"What's troubling you, Son? Are your grades bad, and how about football?"

Sean was disappointed because he really thought his dad would understand. Suddenly he shouted out, "No, Dad, it is Mom!"

"What, Son?"

Sean couldn't imagine why his dad made it so hard for him to discuss this. "I miss her so much, Dad."

All his dad said was, "me too."

Sean had wanted a conversation, not just two words! Before his dad could see a tear dropping from his son's eye, Sean ran upstairs and quickly picked up the phone to dial his girlfriend's number. "Amanda, it's Sean. I really need to talk to you. Suddenly I feel so lost without my mom."

"Ah, Sean, I'm sorry, but I can't talk right now. I am going out," replied Sean's last hope. Click.

"I don't get it. She said she would always be there for me; that no matter what, I could call on her and she would be there for me. I guess that now when I need her the most that doesn't count.

Why do people think that just because Mom died two months ago, I have completely forgotten her and all the numbness has suddenly vanished? Everyone is wrong, and it is really sad that until they experience the death of their own loved one, they will not know how I feel.

If nobody close to me will talk to me about it, who can I turn to? There has to be somebody who can help me. I feel like I am going insane. I honestly don't think anyone understands my problem.

I feel like a suffocating shell is surrounding me, and I am about to break out of that shell. I think I'm going to E-X-P-L-O-D-E! Somebody *please* help me!"

---

**Activity Sheet 10.1.** No Where to Run. Permission is granted to photocopy for grief group use. **Source:** Reprinted from "No Where to Run" by Katie Williams in *Bereavement Magazine* (1992, October). Reprinted with permission of Bereavement Publishing, Inc., October, 1992, 8133 Telegraph Drive, Colorado Springs, CO 80920-7169.

## Activity 10.2. CRAZY GRIEF

**Goal**

To introduce various ways of dealing with feelings.

**Objective**

1. To use an article as a catalyst to discuss the intensity of emotions experienced during the grieving process.

**Introductory Comments**

> Grief can make you feel crazy. Every emotion is let loose and comes flooding in, eroding any sense of balance. The normal routine of the most stable individual can be disrupted by bursting into tears or being totally distracted by the pain of loss. There is no shortcut to make the turmoil disappear. (from "Crazy Grief," Activity Sheet 10.2 [Perschy, 1989])

A primary benefit of a grief group is the chance to acknowledge the intensity of the emotions and how they play havoc in your lives. Stories can be told of crying in the tie department before Father's Day while grieving the death of one's dad, or jealousy while having dinner at a best friend's, watching the friendly bantering, while your own home feels like a morgue without mom. The details may be different, but the frustration and embarrassment of feeling "out of control" have a common thread.

With the guidance of the leaders, the group members can better understand that

intense feelings are normal for the grieving person,
specific feelings are unique to each person,
others may not understand why you react to certain situations as you do, and
there are steps you can take to move through feelings in a healthy way.

**Procedure**

1. Distribute and read copies of the article, "Crazy Grief" (Activity Sheet 10.2). (15 minutes)

2. Use the following questions to promote discussion, keeping in mind that these questions may trigger strong feelings. (30 minutes)

- Can you relate to any part of the article?
- What have been your "crazy grief" experiences?
- Are your friends or family also experiencing "crazy grief"?
- What is the scariest part of grief?
- What helps you deal with the intense feelings?
- How do you feel when you cry in public? Is it okay to cry privately? (Crying has been known to promote healing by providing a release for those pent-up feelings.)
- What advice would *you* give a grieving teen?
- What do you want from other people? How can you let others know what you would like?

3. Follow the discussion with an art or writing activity. Remind the teens to be gentle with themselves.

4. See if the teens can add to the following list of reminders.

### Reminders for Dealing with Difficult Feelings

- **Talk** to a friend, teacher, parent, anyone who can listen without judging you!
- **Write!**
- **Draw, Paint, Work with clay!**
- **Play or listen to music!**
- **Plan fun activities!**
- **Listen to your own feelings** in a caring way.

## Crazy Grief

### by Mary Perschy

Grief can make you feel crazy. Every emotion is let loose and comes flooding in, eroding any sense of balance. The normal routine of the most stable individual can be disrupted by bursting into tears or being totally distracted by the pain or loss. There is no shortcut to make the turmoil disappear.

Wrestling with that grief is the goal of the Teen Support Group sponsored by Hospice Services of Howard County [Columbia, Maryland]. Last October, eight teens ranging in ages from 12 through 16, decided to give this group a try.

The nervousness of the first few sessions melded into a sense of comfort; our group had become a safe place for these teens to move through the grieving process. As my fellow co-leader, Anne Barker, and I approached our sixth meeting, supposedly our last, one group member, Lanisha, asked, "Do we have to stop? I wish this group could go on and on and on." Group members agreed, saying that the group is very important to them in their struggle with loss and they didn't want to lose it, too. Thus, the decision was made to continue the group, meeting twice a month. We agreed to open the group to new members, teens who have experienced the death of someone close to them.

During our first few weeks, we had talked about stages of grief, stress management techniques, and coping strategies during the holidays. We shared our stories about the death of our loved ones and its effect on us. The focus of our eighth meeting was, "What advice would we give a grieving teen?" The teens decided to release themselves from the ground rule of confidentiality in order to include their ideas in this article, wanting their first names used.

The ideas came fast and furiously. "Join a teen grief group to help deal with your feelings," Karyn said. Laurie added with a smile, "Yeah . . . I thought my feelings were dumb and was ashamed of them. Then I came to this group and realized that others have the same feelings. When I am with others outside this group, I feel abnormal. Here I feel more secure. I am a normal grieving person."

Karyn continued, "If there is no group around, choose a friend who you think will stick with you. If you don't have one, find a counselor or psychologist to talk with." This suggestion brought a difference of opinion with one girl saying, "My friends would probably think I was weird for talking about family problems," and another girl, agreeing with the first, saying, "When I get upset, my friends are there. They let me talk and understand my pain. They also help me get my mind off it all."

Emphasizing the need to deal with one's grief, Fame warned, "Don't block it [grief] out of your mind, or it gets worse. I write about how I feel in my journal. I can do it anytime I want, and it helps." Lisa agreed, adding, "When I get worked up over things, I write about it. I go back and read it later and see how differently I feel. It's encouraging to see how far I've come."

After the initial shock of her dad's death wore off, Laurie decided to try out for roles in a musical at school. She's also writing a story about a child with leukemia which she plans to enter into a short story contest. Fame, too, is focusing her energy on writing; her story features a widow.

Lisa listens to music. "I don't feel alone when I listen to sad music. When I'm angry, I like loud music. It reminds me that there are a lot of frustrated people out there."

Skateboarding helps Jeremy work through his aggression. "When I'm angry or sad, it makes me happy." Jason's involvement in lacrosse, soccer, and running gets his mind off his problems.

I was thinking of giving up ballet after my brother died," shared Mandy. "I couldn't hold back the feelings when I danced. I just cried and cried. But now, two months later, I feel good when I dance. Since ballet demands one-track thinking, I can redirect my energy this way. I'm doing something for me."

The variety of responses highlighted the fact that there is no one way to grieve. Each person develops his or her unique style.

The taboo against crying in public was discussed. Even though tears play a normal part in the healing of grief, they can be extremely embarrassing. "I feel so awkward if something reminds me of my dad and I start crying in school," said Laurie. "I head for the bathroom until I stop, at least temporarily." She added, emphatically, "I'd rather cry alone." Everyone readily agreed.

As the topic changed to ways others could be helpful to grieving teens, the energy level in the room intensified as each person waited to describe the incidents that have been frustrating for them.

Underlining the sense of separation that grieving teens experience, much resentment was expressed over comments like, "Aren't you over that yet? Didn't your dad die over a month ago?"

"Some people treat me like I have a disease," said Karyn. "They either totally ignore me or, if they do talk, they are afraid to mention the word 'death,' or the person's name." Others in the group complained about people they hardly knew, seeking information, then passing it on to others without a sense of concern.

"If someone would just say they heard my dad died, and did I want to talk, I would know they cared, yet wouldn't feel pressured to respond," says Karyn. "What really helps is a hug from a friend."

One teen, annoyed that her teacher talked about her dad being sick on a day she was absent said, "It would have been better if the teacher had checked with me first. It was eerie to return to class knowing this information had been shared with kids I hardly knew."

Another teen was offended by her teacher's comment a short while after her dad died. "It's been a month now. You ought to start working on your grades." She explained that it isn't over for her yet. "It is so difficult for me to concentrate. I just wish they could understand."

A favorite analogy of the group is the comparison of grief with a broken leg. People don't expect a person with a broken leg to run a marathon in a month, yet they often expect a grieving person to carry on as if nothing has happened.

Some relatives expect too much. "Now you are the man of the family," said to 14-year-old Jason, infuriated the members of the group. When an adult said, "Take care of your mother," to another girl, she wanted to shout, "What about me?" She explained to the group, "I was afraid they would be shocked by such a selfish statement so I said nothing, but I was seething inside." After describing the incident, she ground her soda bottle into her crackers and slowly articulated, "Don't take my grief away."

It takes courage to grieve in a society that mistakenly values restraint, where we risk the rejection of others by being open and different. Open mourners are a select group, willing to journey into pain and sorrow and anger in order to heal and recover. (Tatelbaum, 1980, p. 9)

I have great respect for the courage of these teens who initially took a risk to join a grief group and are continuing to struggle to maintain some balance amid the chaos of grief. Their desire to be there for other teens has greatly inspired me.

---

**Activity Sheet 10.2.** Crazy Grief. Permission is granted to photocopy for grief group use. **Source:** Reprinted from "Crazy Grief," pp. 1 & 3, by Mary Perschy in *To Make the Road Less Lonely* (1989, Winter) (newsletter).

## Activity 10.3. DEALING WITH ANGER

### Goal

To help teens learn more about anger and how to express it.

### Objectives

1. To identify areas of anger.

2. To increase the repertoire of ways of dealing with angry feelings.

### Introductory Comments

Many grieving persons complain about the intensity of their anger. Anyone can be the target: friends, doctors, nurses, hospital staff, family members, God, or even the person who died. Elisabeth Kubler-Ross, a pioneer in working with dying persons and their families, has conducted workshops for people in transition, many of whom have experienced loss. Kubler-Ross taught that the externalization of negative feelings is essential in working through these feelings and experiencing some release. She encouraged people to pound out their anger and resentment in her workshops. Along with many other health professionals, she believed that pent-up feelings can lead to illness.

Many ways exist of externalizing anger. Aggressive sports help. Vigorously swimming released the intense anger of a 15-year-old boy after his very best friend died of leukemia. Another teen would skateboard by the hour whenever he missed his dad. A tall, slender, agile 16-year-old girl poured her energy into her ballet practices after her brother's suicide.

Of course, punching someone may provide a powerful emotional release; however, the consequences of doing so may bring even more pain. A healthy outlet does not endanger another or oneself. We often remind teens that we do not want to have to move the meeting place to a delinquent shelter because they had chosen risky ways to express their anger.

When the anger is continually destructive, the teen ought to get professional help. There may be more behind the anger, and the teen would need more help than is possible in a group. (See "How to Determine When Additional Help Is Needed" in chapter 14).

### Procedure

1. Tell the teens that for a few minutes we want to explore the questions, "What makes me so angry?"

2. Ask the teens if any of the following quotations sound familiar to them. With each quote, allow the group to explore those angry feelings. Identifying the areas of anger can lead to dealing with the feelings more effectively. (10 minutes)

- "Nothing in my family is the same anymore."
- "'Lighten up,' my friends say. But what do they know? Their dads are still alive and well."
- "I'm angry all the time. I even scare myself. The slightest thing ticks me off. I'm always yelling at my family and my friends. No one wants to be near me."
- "It's all that stupid doctor's fault. Why didn't he find the tumor earlier, before it was too late?"
- "Dad drank beer and ate junk food, day in and day out. He was a real couch potato. He just ignored what everyone said about cholesterol and exercise. His heart just gave out."

3. List the following ways of expressing anger and discuss in the group whether or not each would be effective. (10 minutes)

- Write on paper what angers you, scrunch it up, and throw it into a basket.
- Pound a nerf-type bat at something.
- Go to the bowling alley; give the pins a person's name before you roll the ball.
- Take a half-dozen eggs into the woods; choose a tree and wham the eggs against that tree.
- Scream. Choose a soundproof spot, or those around you may panic and begin imposing restrictions.

4. Ask teens to add other ideas.

5. Depending upon the meeting place, involve the teens in some active expressions of anger, such as scrunching the paper, pounding the air, vigorously flying paper airplanes, drawing an angry picture, listening to angry music, molding a piece of clay with angry movement, or forming clay into an angry figure. (If a group tends to lose control easily, choose less vigorous activities.) (15 to 20 minutes)

# Activity 10.4. DEALING WITH GUILT

## Goal

To help teens learn more about guilt and how to express it.

## Objectives

1. To identify areas of guilt.

2. To explore ways of dealing with guilt feelings.

## Introductory Comments

Feelings of guilt can continue to plague grieving persons, long after the death of someone close. For many, it is more difficult to identify and talk about their guilt than it is their anger. Therefore, these suggestions could fall flat with little or no response. Some teens may be ready, however, to address these issues of guilt.

Guilt feelings often accompany grief. Death is final. The survivors cannot complete that last disagreement. The "I love you" goes unsaid. The "I'm sorry" is unspoken. The embraces, the good times, are no longer a part of our lives. Sometimes the ending is abrupt.

How can we help teens grapple with guilt as they put their relationship with the person who has died into perspective? These activities are designed to help teens pinpoint the causes of the guilt feelings, determine whether or not they were truly at fault, and explore various ways of moving through the pain.

## Procedure

1. Tell the teens that for a few minutes we want to explore, "What is there to be guilty about?"

2. Read these two sample scenarios to the teens or, if appropriate, use an example from your own life.

- "I wasn't there when my mom died. None of us were. Dad and I went home to shower and take a break after being at the hospital for two days straight. Then she died. I just feel terrible that I wasn't there."

- "My dad always yelled at me when I stayed out late. Saturday he called me a no-good tramp. He had been drinking. I screamed back at him. I told him that I hated his guts. That night he had a heart attack. I cannot forgive myself."

3. Ask the teens if they can recall stories of people feeling guilty after someone died. (For example, in the movie *Ordinary People*, the brother felt guilty that he lived and that his brother died.)

4. Talk about the fact that many people have guilt feelings after someone dies.

5. Remind teens that talking about guilt can be embarrassing; therefore, the ground rule of confidentiality must be maintained. As the leader, set the tone by sharing a personal issue or a comment such as, "I've heard of bereaved persons who shared harsh words with their loved ones before they died and wound up regretting it long afterwards." Activity 10.4 gives us a chance to recall those moments of regret and learn how to move beyond the guilt.

6. Make copies of the open-ended statements ("I Wish I Had . . . I Wish I Hadn't . . .") in Activity Sheet 10.4 and distribute them to the teens to complete. **Note:** The amount of time for this activity will vary greatly from group to group.

7. Provide time for those who wish to talk about their experiences. If no one chooses to share, encourage them to talk with a trusted adult or friend at another time or possibly write about the experiences.

8. Tell the teens that now we want to explore, "Am I truly to blame?"

9. Help the teens determine whether or not they were really blameworthy. Have them ask themselves, "Did I truly have control over the situation, or am I assuming guilt for something I could not help?" The following scenarios may offer some clarity.

- "I let my friend use my car. If only I had said no, then he would be here now." (You made the decision to lend your car based upon what you knew then. You cannot hold yourself responsible for the drunk driver who ran into your friend.)
- "Mom died without me being there." (You were incapable of keeping a vigil for days without collapsing. Some persons need to be alone in order to die.)
- "If only I could have done more. Should I have nagged dad to go see a doctor for his headaches? I never even checked on him the night that he died of an aneurism." (People have headaches for many reasons. You didn't know how serious this one was, nor did anyone else in your family.)

10. As the teens respond to these scenarios and their own answers to "I Wish I Had . . . I Wish I Hadn't . . ." (Activity Sheet 10.4), help them determine what was beyond their control and what reflects their true actions.

11. Tell the teens that now we want to spend a few minutes exploring "Ways to Move Beyond the Guilt." As the teens become better able to distinguish between guilt feelings of inadequacy when unable to control the situation, and a true sense of blame, the following sections can help them deal with the feelings.

### a   When we feel guilty for what we couldn't control . . .

Things happen that are beyond our control. We are human and, therefore, limited. It is inappropriate to assume the blame for something that is impossible. We are incapable of predicting the future, running someone else's life, or being with one person indefinitely. When you know that the situation was beyond your control, and yet you still feel guilty, it may help to

- remind yourself that you did the best you could,
- write affirmations that fit your particular issue (e.g., "I cannot tell the future," or "I cannot control another person's life."), or
- talk with a nonjudgmental friend or counselor to put it into perspective.

### b   When our guilt feelings reflect our true actions . . .

When you recognize that you have said some things and acted in ways that you wish you had not, it is normal to feel guilty. We need to come to grips with the reality of the human condition. Each person is imperfect, and we all make mistakes. We now have the opportunity to forgive ourselves, to offer ourselves the same compassion that we often give to another. These suggestions may help you in beginning to move through the feelings:

- Write a letter to the person who has died, expressing your regrets. Then, write another letter as you picture your loved one responding to you in a compassionate way. Continue the correspondence. Discuss with the group, a friend, or counselor any insights that you have received.
- Some issues may be deep, longstanding, and may require help from a professional counselor or a guide trained in a spiritual discipline consistent with your own.

## I Wish I Had . . . I Wish I Hadn't . . .

If only I had . . .

If only I hadn't . . .

It was my fault when . . .

I'm so sorry that . . .

I still cannot forgive her for . . .

I can't forgive myself for . . .

If we had one more day together, I would . . .

---

**Activity Sheet 10.4.** Open-ended statements. Permission is granted to photocopy for grief group use.

## Activity 10.5. FOCUSING: BEING WITH FEELINGS IN A CARING WAY

**Note:** Know your community as to whether or not these words (bio-spirituality) and/or activities would be offensive to some people. If so, choose a different activity.

### Goal

To guide a teen through **bio-spiritual focusing.**

### Objectives

1. To encourage the teen to be compassionate toward himself or herself while listening to difficult feelings.

2. To help a teen be with difficult feelings in a caring way, allowing the story to unfold and some resolution to occur.

### Introductory Comments

People often want to run from the painful feelings of grief and sometimes choose to take a temporary break. However, an important part of grief is to experience the pain in order to move toward some resolution or healing.

The process of bio-spiritual focusing is a valuable tool in assisting persons struggling with intense feelings. A trained guide leads a person in a nonintrusive manner, encouraging that person (focuser) to be with the felt-sense of the emotion. The focuser could hold a pillow or stuffed animal against the part of the body where the feeling is located, such as the tight stomach, or the tense neck. This caring-feeling presence is being offered not to take the feeling away, nor to change it, but to allow the story behind it to unfold. The skilled guide, then, continues to accompany the focuser through this healing process.

Although many video and written resources are available on bio-spiritual focusing, the best way to help teens is by first being guided yourself through the process with the help of someone who already knows it. In this way you learn the process from inside your own experience, rather than just reading a description of a technique. It is your own body knowledge of bio-spiritual focusing that is your best teacher. There are programs throughout the world, and many in the U.S., that provide an opportunity to experience this simple, but extremely effective, process.

Information on available programs can be found in the Resource Material section of this book.

## Activity 10.6. EXPRESSING GRIEF THROUGH VISUAL ARTS

### Goal

To explore with the teens various ways of expressing grief through visual arts.

### Objectives

1. By participating in painting, molding clay, and drawing, teens can learn to be with difficult feelings and move through them.

2. To help increase the self-esteem of grieving teens by encouraging them to use their creative abilities.

### Introductory Comments

Kathie explained that she is not a very verbal person, so her art is the easiest way for her to express herself. "I get lost in my art and paint for hours and hours," she said.

After her husband died, she recalled, "I knew I was suffering, I needed to paint. I had to see the anger; visualize the anger. It was like admitting, 'Yes, *I am* angry.' However, I didn't want anyone else to see it," she admitted. "Sometimes I would become embarrassed, and I would try to change the painting so it wouldn't look angry. Then it looked like it had makeup on it. It was no longer true."

Eventually, 20 paintings later, the paintings were happier. As she looked at a woman floating with arms outstretched, Kathie was surprised to see how different this painting was compared to the earlier ones.

Although Kathie is an adult, expressing feelings through art can be helpful at any age. Artistic expression allows us to connect with what is real within ourselves. As we create what resonates with our inner truth, we can move more freely through the pain of our difficult feelings.

### Procedure

These are only a few ideas for engaging the teens in expression through art. Other ideas may flow from the discussion.

#### Painting Images of Feelings (15 to 20 minutes).

1.  Say to the teens, "Notice how you are feeling."
2.  Identify one feeling.

3. Look at the colors of markers or paints and choose a color that matches how you feel.
4. Draw a picture, or just allow your brush or marker to move in any free-flowing way.
5. Add other colors if you wish. Stay with the feeling
6. Reflect upon what you drew.
7. Share with another teen in your drawing/painting and your feelings.

## Creating Memory Beads (20 to 30 minutes).

1. Have the teens design memory beads to highlight the special times the teen had with the person who died.
2. Explain the importance of remembering these times by making a symbol of their connectedness.
3. Encourage the teens to recall what they liked about the person who has died—their specialness. Or have them recall an event they would like to memorialize.
4. Provide acrylic paints, tiny brushes, beads with holes, and yarn to string the completed beads.
5. Encourage them to do additional beads, if it seems right to do more than one.
6. Walk among the teens as they make their memory beads. As you move about, ask the teen to describe their design and help describe the memory.
7. Allow time for those who wish to talk about their creation.
8. Brainstorm ideas of what they could do with these beads.

## Allowing the Clay to Speak (30 to 40 minutes).

1. Say to the teens that the soft wet feel of molding a piece of clay can help you reflect and connect with how you are feeling.
2. Make suggestions as they work. The following suggestions may be used or more ideas may evolve. Allow time afterwards to talk about the experience.

- Just continue molding, allowing a rhythm to develop.
- Pound the clay angrily, if that is how you feel. Or just stay with the lonely, sad, or content feelings (or whatever unfolds) as you move the clay.
- Make a symbol that matches how you feel (e.g., a flame to represent the fire of anger, a bowl to portray the feeling of emptiness, or a rock to symbolize numbness). You could be with your object in a caring way or decide to smash it. Go with how you feel.
- Create a memory of the person who has died similar to the memory beads. Attempt to "be with" what you have created.
- Share with the group what touched you the most.

## Activity 10.7. WRITE THROUGH GRIEF

**Goal**

To help teens use writing as a tool for working through the feelings of grief.

**Objectives**

1. To encourage teens to use writing to express their feelings.

2. To suggest ways to commemorate special days by writing to the person who has died.

3. To provide a safe atmosphere for teens to explore various writing forms and share their work within the group.

**Introductory Comments**

The middle-of-the-night darkness that often accompanies grief can be unyielding. Who is there to listen to your bizarre conglomeration of feelings? There may be a trusted friend who is willing to be awakened, to be with you as you deal with your pain. However, this willingness often is short-lived. Life must go on.

How can I be listened to? A simple spiral notebook or an elaborate cloth-covered one can be a wonderful help in working through the craziness of grief. The blank page is always available, will not judge you, and allows you the freedom to be yourself and say whatever you please.

In journaling workshops, participants are encouraged to write as they speak. For grieving persons, it is a powerful way to recall the good times and the not-so-good times. It can be that opportunity to bring closure to what was unfinished.

In her pamphlet "Write Grief: How to Transform Loss with Writing," Gail Jacobsen (1990) encouraged grieving persons to write as a great way of organizing their thoughts.

> You will gain insights about your feelings, fears and concerns; the more you become aware of your thoughts and choices, the better your judgments will become as you reassemble your shattered life. Overwhelming concerns will become manageable, thoughts less fragmented. Healing will occur both from the writing and from the reflection upon the writing. (p. 5)

Jacobsen confided that she had wanted answers to why there was death, loss, and grief. Finding no suitable answers to the question "why," she turned her focus to answer "how" you grieve. Eventually, she found that writing enfolded and transformed her grief.

Some teens find writing helpful in exploring their feelings and working them through. Other teens may be less inclined to write.

## Procedure

1. Provide simple notebooks for teens to use as journals. Allow time for them to personalize their covers by decorating them.

2. Encourage teens to write in their journals when they feel the need to talk about the crazy feelings of grief and there is no one available to listen. Remind them not to worry about correct grammar or punctuation. Just let the words flow onto the paper.

3. In anticipation of an anniversary, birthday, holiday, or other important day, encourage the teens to write to the person who has died as if they were speaking to him or her. Provide some ideas to write about such as the following:

   • update your loved one on what is happening in your own life;
   • write about something you wished you had said or done;
   • say how you have felt since the person has died; and
   • write about how other family members are doing.

4. Encourage the teens to experiment with different writing forms, such as poetry, stories about the person's life, or phrases the person who has died used to use. They even could add some drawings to the writing or add some words to a drawing.

5. Invite the teens to share their journal entries if they feel comfortable doing so.

6. Throughout other sessions, remind the teens to write about certain issues or feelings that have been mentioned.

# Activity 10.8. EXPRESSING GRIEF THROUGH MUSIC

## Goal

To expose teens to music as a means of working through their feelings.

## Objectives

1. To encourage teens to listen to music when they would like to change their moods.

2. To support teens as they use music that matches their feelings to explore those feelings.

## Introductory Comments

While being interviewed about what helped teens deal with their feelings of grief, one young woman said that she listened to music. "I don't feel so alone when I listen to sad music. When I'm angry, I like loud music. It reminds me that there are a lot of frustrated people out there."

Music can have a powerful influence on our emotions and even on our bodies. Research conducted by Helen Bonny showed that music lowered patients' heart rate and blood pressure, and significantly changed emotions from negative to positive on the Emotional Rating Scale (Merritt, 1996, p. 127).

Grieving persons could make use of music both to **connect with the feelings** and to go on to **change the feelings** when desired.

**Music Can Help Us Be with Our Difficult Feelings.** An important task of grieving is to "be with" the painful feelings. Often the demands of daily living consume our attention, and we forge ahead, ignoring the screams of the anger, the loneliness, or the guilt feelings.

Yet, our numbed, emotional life can be unthawed, and we can recapture our zest for living. First, we need to acknowledge, and be with, whatever feelings we find. Although unpleasant initially, entering into the struggle can heal the pain.

**Music Can Assist Us in Letting Our Feelings Flow.**

> When conditions seem too frightening to let out your feelings, you can invite music's gentle nudge to help you express them. As you allow the music to help you experience pain and sadness, all the locked-up joy bursts forth too, releasing a vitality that kindles interest and excitement in all aspects of your life, your work, your relationships, your studies. (Merritt, 1996, p. 27)

**Music Can Relax, Renew, and Soothe.** There are times when we cannot take time out to listen to our feelings and allow their full expression: The assignment needs to be completed, the Scholastic Achievement Test (SAT) is scheduled for tomorrow morning, the customers at the clothing store we work at want our undivided attention. Music can help us temporarily change our mood.

**Music Can Stimulate or Calm Us.** "If the tempo gets faster, our hearts will beat faster," according to Stephanie Merritt. "If you want to calm down, you would use music with a slower tempo" (Merritt, 1996, p. 121).

Merritt also suggested that

> [i]f you are feeling edgy, irritable, or hyper, start with a piece of music that is not too quiet, so that you are able to resonate with it and perhaps give some of your anxiety over to the music. Later, you can switch to a more tranquil piece of music. (Merritt, 1996, p. 147)

Since each person is unique, have the teens listen to a piece and jot down their emotions.

## Procedure

1. Demonstrate how music can change our moods. Use music from a favorite movie or ask teens to bring in CDs or audiotapes of a favorite songs. (Although most teens would know enough to not choose one with profanity, it would be well to set boundaries on what is acceptable to bring.)

2. Play a selection. Ask the group to write words or draw about how they feel physically and emotionally. Talk about it.

3. Continue to vary the music. Ask teens to keep track of how they feel upon listening to each selection.

4. Encourage the teens to listen to various pieces at home for five minutes a piece and then write down how they feel (Activity Sheet 10.8).

5. Have teens arrange their list of emotions into categories that could include, but not be limited to, anger, sadness, calmness, excitement.

6. At the next meeting, listen to the teens' selections.

7. Ask the group members to share responses and add to their lists.

8. Discuss the possible uses of such a list to "match our feelings" and to allow our feelings to be expressed, and to change the feelings to provide a better balance in our daily lives.

9. During the discussion, weave in the fact that this may not be an effective tool for everyone. Also, the change could be very slight. Of course, listening to music cannot be a substitute for seeing a mental health professional when the low feeling is intense and has been present for a long time.

**Note:** Be concerned and prepared to provide additional professional help when depressed teens choose to listen extensively to hard metal rock or if the music of choice has only negative lyrics. When the teens experience such deep, dark emotions for long periods of time, they may have difficulty moving beyond these emotions and may become suicidal. As the leader, you need to advise these teens to meet regularly with a mental health professional. A parent should be notified if a teen is suicidal.

**Note:** There is a wide range of time that groups could spend on this activity; therefore, no specific time is indicated.

## Expressing Grief through Music

### Music Can Affect How We Feel

**Stay with Feelings.** When you feel the intensity of your grief, take some time to be alone. Choose music that matches your feelings. Stay with it. Be with the feelings in a caring way. You also can draw, paint, write, or move around. Then create your own music on an instrument, or makeshift ones such as pots and pans, spoons, wooden blocks, or any nonbreakable objects around the house.

You could finish by listening to calming music to give yourself a better balance. Write about the experience in your journal, or talk to a trusted person.

**Balance Your Moods.** You also can change your feelings. If you feel low, and wish to have more energy, play something with a faster beat. When you wish to relax, choose something slower. Consult your Music List below when choosing a piece.

### Music List

Since each of us responds in our own unique way, listen to your favorite pieces of music. Before each begins, jot down how you feel; then jot down how you feel again after you have listened. Continue the list on the back of this paper or in your journal.

| Name of Selection | Before | After |
|---|---|---|
|  |  |  |

**Note:** If you constantly are drawn toward playing hard metal rock for long periods of time, a word of caution. You may have difficulty moving beyond the intensity of the feelings while connecting with this music. There are concerns that such music may increase suicidal tendencies. A teen hotline or a mental health professional would be helpful in moving you beyond the pain that draws you to consistently choose only intense music. Therefore, limit hard metal rock with negative lyrics and vary your musical selections.

---

**Activity Sheet 10.8.** Expressing Grief through Music. Permission is granted to photocopy for grief group use.

# Activity 10.9. MEMORIALIZING A LOVED ONE IN A FABRIC WALLHANGING OR QUILT

**Goal**

To enable teens to create a tangible memorial of a loved one.

**Objective**

1. To design and create a fabric creation within a group setting to celebrate the life of a loved one.

**Procedure**

1. Ask teens to think about the person who has died. What words or symbols could be used to represent that person?

2. Encourage teens to capture the impression of that person in a drawing.

3. Using muslin squares and fabric pens, have teens draw that picture on the fabric.

4. For those who wish to make the fabric into an individual wallhanging, the top could be rolled over and stitched. A wooden dowel could be put through the hem with a piece of yarn connecting each end.

5. If teens wish to create a group quilt, each teen can complete a square representing his or her loved one. With the teens' permission, incorporate the spares into a group quilt to represent all their loved ones. Ask a quilter to assist in combining the squares. Take a picture of the quilt, and send it to each participant. The teens could gather for a reunion or a memorial service to see the quilt and commemorate the lives of their loved ones.

# Chapter 11

# REMEMBERING THE PERSON WHO DIED

A special person has died. This person has had an impact upon one's life, and that influence will live through that person long after the person is buried. An important step in working through grief is to commemorate the life of the person who has died. As teens tell their stories and share mementos, they are encouraged to make this person real for the group in order to better appreciate the gifts that person has shared. It is important to include a variety of activities in planning the sessions, beginning with "Telling One's Story," Activity 11.1, during the first or second meeting. Activity 11.2, "Sharing a Memento," or some part of Activity 11.3, "Commemorating a Special Life," could be scheduled toward the end of the sessions.

If the timing of the group coincides with the celebration of a holiday, several ideas are offered to prepare for those special days. Often teens complain of a sense of dread, recalling earlier family celebrations when the deceased loved one was present. Advance planning can help teens and their families choose what part of it they wish to keep and what part they wish to change. This conscious effort even may contain a way to memorialize this person who had died. Often this frees those who remain to speak about the person without fear of offending anyone.

## Activity 11.1. TELLING ONE'S STORY

### Goal

To make the death of a loved one real and to better accept the loss.

### Objectives

1. To encourage teens to focus on the circumstances of the death of their loved one and how it has affected them.

2. To encourage teens to share their reflections to lessen their sense of isolation.

### Introductory Comments

After a person dies, there is a need for the loved ones to repeat the details about the dying process over and over to each new person who may have known the deceased.

Sharing one's story is a very important part of the grieving process. It is a way to make it more believable, that is, to know that the death really took place.

As we each tell our story, parts of another person's story may connect with our own story, while other parts will be different. Death becomes less scary when we talk about the circumstances and listen to each other's stories. We learn once again that it is all right to feel the many emotions that are a part of grief.

### Procedure

1. Distribute copies of the questions in Activity Sheet 11.1 or just write the questions on a chart.

2. Add other questions if you or the teens so desire.

3. Use the questions to help the teens focus upon the details around the death of their loved one. (25 to 35 minutes)

4. To help set the stage for sharing stories, a peer facilitator or a leader could speak of a personal experience of grief. This provides a model for sharing.

5. Allow time for each person to tell his or her story.

6. Follow up by listing the many emotions mentioned in the sharing.

7. Use this list at a later meeting when discussing the feelings of grief.

**Note:** There can be a wide range of time allotted for this activity.

## Telling One's Story

These questions may be helpful in recalling events around the death of your loved one. If it helps, jot down notes.

1. Who died? How did he or she die?

2. Was it a short or long time ago?

3. How did you find out that your loved one died? Who told you?

4. What was your immediate reaction after hearing of the death?

5. How do you feel now?

6. Did you see your loved one after the death?

7. What was that like for you to see (or not see) your loved one?

8. Was there a funeral, shiva, or other kind of memorial?

9. Were you involved in the service?

10. What parts were really difficult?

11. What parts were okay?

12. What memory of the person who has died makes you feel good?

---

**Activity Sheet 11.1.** Telling One's Story. Permission is granted to photocopy for grief group use.

# Activity 11.2. SHARING A MEMENTO

## Goal

To remember the person who has died.

## Objectives

1. To discuss the importance of remembering the person who has died.

2. To share an item or a memory with the group.

## Introductory Comments

Taking time to talk about someone who is no longer in our lives is a very important part of the grieving process, but who will listen? (This may be a good time to set up a phone tree, so that the teens could call each other the night or two before the next meeting to remind one another about bringing something.)

Ask each teen if he or she has some memento of the person who has died. It could be something that the person owned or something that reminds the teen of that person. If the teen has nothing at hand, ask him or her to recall a memory.

## Procedure

1. Allow time for each person to speak about his or her memento. If someone forgot to bring an item, ask that teen to recall an event, a character trait, or something special about the person who has died. This discussion could evolve into how this person has contributed to the life of the teen. (20 to 30 minutes)

2. Ask the teens to think of someone to share these memories with. Suggest that they continue the process of "remembering."

# Activity 11.3. COMMEMORATING A SPECIAL LIFE

## Goal

To help teens appreciate the value of commemorating the life of the person who has died.

## Objectives

1. To help the teens learn practical ways of recalling the life of their loved one.

2. To encourage the teens to find their own ways of commemorating the life of their loved one and their special relationship with that person.

## Introductory Comments

Sandra Fox (1988), who worked extensively with grieving children, encouraged grieving persons to commemorate the life of the person who has died.

Many families provide some ritual shortly after the person has died, based upon their religious or ethnic tradition. Some teens may have been involved in the planning and enactment of these services. Others simply may have been observers.

Since this ritual may have been the first of its kind for a particular teen, it may have generated feelings of awkwardness.

## Procedure

1. Make copies of Activity Sheet 11.3., page 1, and distribute them to the teens or simply weave the questions from Activity Sheet 11.3, page 1, into a discussion about the importance of commemorating the special lives of our loved ones. (20 to 30 minutes)

2. A session of the grief group could be set aside to commemorate. Bring in an object that may be a reminder of the person who has died. Then share information about this object. (See Activity 11.2., "Sharing a Memento.")

3. Make copies of Activity Sheet 11.3, page 2, and distribute them to the teens.

4. Have the teens respond to these open-ended questions.

5. Discuss teens' responses to the questions in Activity Sheet 11.3, page 2. (20 to 30 minutes)

6. Share with the teens the "Simple Ways of Recalling a Special Life" listed here. More ideas are available in "Expressing Grief through Visual Arts," Activity 10.6.

### Writing

our favorite times
what I miss the most
when I was very young
a biography of part of the person's life

### Drawing

events
places
any memories or other ideas

### Creating

an album, using photos and memorabilia
a musical composition
a dance

## Commemorating a Special Life, Part A

1. What kind of ritual, if any, took place after your loved one died?

2. What part was meaningful; what was not?

3. Did you know the purpose behind the activity? (The purpose of such customs, as viewing the body, helps to make the loss real, which is an important part of the grieving process.)

4. Other rituals may be planned on birthdays, or on the anniversary of the person's death. It may include many persons connected with the one who has died, or it may just be a few persons. Has your family planned or been invited to any rituals for your loved one? If so, describe the ritual.

---

**Activity Sheet 11.3, page 1.** Commemorating a Special Life, Part A. Permission is granted to photocopy for grief group use.

**Commemorating a Special Life, Part B**

1. My favorite memory of my was when  _____

_____

_____

2. I am happy that we had a chance to  _____

_____

_____

3. I wish that we could have  _____

_____

_____

4. A not-so-favorite memory was when  _____

_____

_____

5. I remember laughing together when  _____

_____

_____

6. A legacy that my loved one left me is  _____

_____

_____

**Activity Sheet 11.3, page 2.** Commemorating a Special Life, Part B. Permission is granted to photocopy for grief group use.

# Activity 11.4. HOLIDAYS AND GRIEF

## Goal

To prepare for the changes in celebrating the holidays without the person who has died.

## Objectives

1. To provide a framework for acknowledging the fact that the traditions of holiday times may be altered because of the death of a significant person in the family.

2. To tailor this year's celebration to the reality of the changes.

## Introductory Comments

Holiday traditions typically are passed from generation to generation, or they are created fresh out of the relationships of being together. Whether we eat crabs on the porch of a beach house every August, decorate a Christmas tree amid the smell of hot cider, recall the plight of our ancestors at the family Seder, or light the candles amid the joyous songs of Kwanza, holidays typify the celebration of family togetherness. We belong. There is a sense of being special.

Yes, we have many memories, and often we look forward to next year's celebration.

Then, a key figure dies. The anticipation now is clouded. Who will lead the Seder now that Grandpa has died? Who even wants to celebrate Thanksgiving now that Mom is gone? With a sense of dread, the days tick away and the holiday is upon us.

Those around us prepare with excitement, which only intensifies our grief.

Admitting our anxiety about the coming event can be the first step in creating a healthy way of dealing with the "crazy feelings" of grief around holiday time.

## Procedure

1. Read through the open-ended sentences in Activity Sheet 11.4, page 1. Add other appropriate questions. Make copies and distribute them to the teens.

2. Discuss the teens' responses to the open-ended sentences. (20 to 30 minutes)

3. Use an art activity to help the teens visualize the event and better prepare for it. For example, ask the teens to do the following: Fold a sheet of paper. On one half of the sheet, draw a picture of how you celebrated a holiday before your loved one died. On the other half, draw how you expect to celebrate this year. (If it has been more than one year since a

teen's loved one has died, the paper could be folded into thirds. That teen could draw the "before picture," the first celebration after the death, and the approaching holiday.)

4. Provide time for the teens to share their drawings with the group. It may be easier to have them talk with a partner first.

5. Help the teens decide on what suggestions they would make if a family planning meeting was held about celebrating the holiday. Look at Activity Sheet 11.4, page 2, for additional ideas. Help them to be specific.

6. Encourage the teens to talk with other family members about preparing for the holidays.

7. Encourage participation in a family meeting. Well in advance of the holidays, the leaders of the parent group could suggest that the parent(s) call the family together to get some input about how to celebrate this year.

8. Share copies of the ideas from Activities 11.1 and 11.2 with the adult(s) to help plan the meeting. The meeting can be as simple or as complex as the adult wishes, depending upon the maturity and particular needs of each family member. The items on Activity Sheet 11.4, page 2, may serve as discussion starters.

9. Copy Activity Sheet 11.4, page 2, and distribute it to the teens. Let them know that their ideas are important and will be shared with adults in their life if the teens approve doing so. (30 minutes)

10. Have teens discuss their responses to Activity Sheet 11.4, page 2.

11. Distribute copies of "Holidays and Grief, Part C: Tips for Getting through Extended Holidays," Activity Sheet 11.4, page 3, and discuss the ideas with the teens. (15 minutes)

## Holidays and Grief, Part A

1. My favorite holiday has been _____

_____

2. My greatest loss has been _____

_____

3. This holiday I am worried about_____

_____

4. What I fear the most is _____

_____

5. I hope _____

_____

6. I wish I could _____

_____

7. I am surprised that I feel so _____

_____

**Activity Sheet 11.4, page 1.** Holidays and Grief, Part A. Permission is granted to photocopy for grief group use.

**Holidays and Grief, Part B**

1. My favorite part of (name the holiday) was _____

_____

2. I hope this year we still _____

_____

3. I will miss (deceased person), particularly when we _____

_____

4. I would like us to change _____

_____

5. I would like to do the following special something together to commemorate the life of (the deceased person) during the holidays _____

_____

6. I would rather commemorate (the deceased person's) life in my own private way ____

_____

**Activity Sheet 11.4, page 2.** Holidays and Grief, Part B. Permission is granted to photocopy for grief group use.

## Holidays and Grief, Part C

### Tips for Getting through Extended Holidays

When you are on an extended holiday and have a block of time with little or no structure, the situation can be a source of anxiety. Remember to do the following:

**Eat Balanced Meals.** Although there may be many sweets available, balance them with fruits and vegetables. Too much sugar can create the "sugar blues." A grieving person doesn't need these feelings intensified.

**Exercise Wisely.** Enjoy your sports, but don't overdo it. Know when to rest. If you are not into sports, begin by doing something simple like taking nature walks. Gradually add more activity. The endorphins produced by vigorous activity can lift your spirits and give yourself renewed energy.

**Plan Fun Things.** If your family cannot enjoy the fun, spend some of the holiday with others who can. Plan ahead. Contact people and be specific about time and place. Some structure each day can give you a balance. Beware, however, of using alcohol or drugs. The long-term effects can be destructive.

**Plan Time with Someone Who Will Let You Talk about Your Loved One, If You Wish.** Sometimes, people are uncomfortable when the name of the deceased person is mentioned. You will get a sense of who feels comfortable when you talk about your loved one.

**Plan a Project.** Repair your bike, paint your room, or just rearrange the furniture. Work on a school assignment with a friend.

**Invite over a New Friend.** Rent a movie. Play a video game. Do a craft project.

**Examine Your Support System.** Is there someone you can call if you are feeling overwhelmed? Know the crisis hotline number in case you are alone and need to talk.

**Plan to Be Good to Yourself.** List five things you could do to pamper yourself:
1.
2.
3.
4.
5.

---

**Activity Sheet 11.4, page 3.** Holidays and Grief, Part C: Tips for Getting through Extended Holidays. Permission is granted to photocopy for grief group use.

# Chapter 12

# COMPLETING THE GROUP EXPERIENCE

These final four activities allow for time to close the group. When a group has bonded successfully, the members need time to complete their time together. Activity 12.1, "Supports in My Life," fulfills a twofold purpose. It gives the teens an opportunity to examine their own support system in order to evaluate the extent of support they already have and how they may need to expand it. The leaders can observe each teen's profile of support to see if he or she has a strong enough network. The leaders may speak to the teens of the advantages of seeking professional help when one has a very limited support system.

"Saying Good-bye" (Activity 12.4) allows the teens to write something positive about each of the other teens. This affirmation is very reassuring to the teens as they prepare to end the group.

Just as some groups began with the throwing and catching of a ball in "Getting to Know You" (Activity 7.1), some groups may end with a similar experience. "Reflections about the Group" (Activity 12.3) offers the opportunity to talk about what the group meant and what group members will take from the group within the same framework.

# Activity 12.1. SUPPORTS IN MY LIFE

## Goal

To provide a structure to help teens examine their support system and determine whether or not they need to be expanded.

## Objectives

1. Encourage teens to identify what persons are supportive of them and what interests and activities are meaningful to them.

2. Help teens decide if, at times, they may need more support, such as a professional counselor, and how to find one who can help them.

## Introductory Comments

This exercise is valuable toward the end of the group sessions to make sure each teen has a satisfactory network when the group is ended.

A **network** includes the persons in our lives who care about us and support us in good times and difficult times. In return, we support them. Our activities and belongings, along with our network of people, give meaning to our lives.

## Procedure

1. Make copies of Activity Sheet 12.1., "Supports in My Life," and ask each teen to fill it in.

2. Talk about the responses.

3. Explore with the teens how they could broaden their network, if more support would be helpful. Challenge the teens to think about persons they could add to their support system. This could include teachers, counselors, clergy, rabbis—people whom they could trust.

4. Speak of the value of seeing a mental health professional when feeling overwhelmed or depressed for long periods of time and how to go about finding the right one.

5. Provide a hotline phone number and leaders' phone numbers for crisis calls. (30 to 40 minutes)

### Supports in My Life

A healthy support system is important, especially while we are grieving. This list may help identify who is there for you and what things give you energy. Fill in the specifics.

**People Who Care about Me**

friends:

family:

relatives:

neighbors:

teachers:

counselor/mental health professional:

minister/priest/rabbi:

**Interests That Are Important to Me**
school related:
church:
work:
sports:
arts/crafts:
other:

**Things That Are Important to Me**
pets:
memorabilia (pictures, special items):

**People I Could Add to This List to Strengthen My Network**
1.
2.
3.

**When a crisis occurs, and your support persons are not available, call the local hotline number. (Record number here:                     )**

---

**Activity Sheet 12.1.** Supports in My Life. Permission is granted to photocopy for grief group use.

# Activity 12.2. CLOSING CEREMONY OF TRIBUTE

## Goal

To appreciate within the group setting the person who has died.

## Objectives

1. To acknowledge the gifts of the person who has died.

2. To move toward closure within the group as members make their special person more real by recalling the memories.

## Procedure

1. Make the room dark. Light a candle. Ask the teens to spend time thinking of the person who has died. What were the special traits? What will I remember the most? When I hear that persons's name, I recall. . . . When I think of that person, I feel. . . .

2. Think of an image or symbol that matches any thought or feeling from procedure 1. Spend time making that image real.

3. Provide a time for describing memories or images of the person who has died. Allow enough time for teens to share more than once, if they wish.

4. Close with a moment of silent thanksgiving for the life of this person. (20 to 30 minutes)

# Activity 12.3. REFLECTIONS ABOUT THE GROUP

**Goal**

To provide closure for the group members.

**Objectives**

1. To provide an opportunity for the teens to reflect upon the impact that the group had upon them.

2. To share what they learned with the group members.

**Procedure**

1. Just as an earlier activity gathered the teens in a circle and had them respond to a question, close in a similar manner. Allow them time to ponder the open-ended statements below. Pause after each round. Anyone is allowed to pass. (20 minutes)

- One thing I learned about grief was . . .
- What I will remember is . . .
- One thing I would change about the group is . . .
- What I appreciated the most was . . .

## Activity 12.4. SAYING GOOD-BYE

**Goal**

To emphasize the value of each person's presence in the group.

**Objectives**

1. To affirm each participant in writing.

2. To end the group in a positive tone.

**Procedure**

1. There are two varieties to this activity. If the group is excitable, the first may be more fitting. If the teens need some movement, the second provides that outlet.

   a   Ask each group member (including leaders) to write his or her name on the top of a sheet of paper. Pass the papers in one consistent direction. Each person is asked to write a good-bye note to that person or something positive about that person. When the sheets reach the person whose name is on the top, each participant is encouraged to read the remarks and breathe in the positive energy.

OR

   b   Paper plates are taped to the back of each participant. Everyone has an opportunity to write something positive about each person on that person's plate. The ending is the same as above.

2. Offer the opportunity for any last words.

3. Teens could be invited back to join the next group as regular participants or as peer facilitators. Peer facilitators could lead the "Helping Teens Connect" (chapter 7) activities. They could be the first to share in order to model a way of responding. New teens often are more comfortable watching other teens lead.

4. If a group has bonded particularly well, consider a reunion group and make plans.

5. Have additional roster lists available and remind the teens that they can call one another.

# PART C
# EVALUATION AND FOLLOW-UP

Sample evaluations provided in chapter 13 are designed to assist leaders in developing their own evaluation tools according to the particular activities they used with a given group. Many organizations require an evaluation of their groups to provide feedback for future planning.

Leaders will need to read the section in chapter 14 entitled "How to Determine When Additional Help Is Needed." If leaders read this during the early sessions of the group, they are better able to be attentive all along to the warning signs for a person considering suicide. Other conditions for making a referral to a mental health professional are highlighted in chapter 14 as well.

Chapter 14 also provides a variety of ideas for keeping in touch with the teens once the group sessions are over.

# Chapter 13

# EVALUATION

An evaluation is a valuable way of finding out what was helpful and what was not helpful. Talking about the various items within the group gives the leaders a better sense of why some activities work better than others.

Many approaches can be utilized in constructing an evaluation form. Figures 13.1, 13.2, and 13.3 are three examples of evaluation forms that have been used over the past several years, each of which takes teens about 20 minutes to fill out.

**Evaluation #1**

# TEEN GRIEF GROUP—(HOSPICE SERVICES)

Your evaluation of what we did in the grief group can be very helpful for us as we plan future groups.

**Directions:** Please answer: yes, because . . . or no, because . . .

Did you like:

1. time we met_____

2. place we met  _____

3. number of persons in group  _____

4. how the leaders treated you_____

5. Which topics were helpful to you?


    stages of grief  _____

    changes caused by grief  _____

**Figure 13.1, page 1.** Sample evaluation #1.

journaling _____

stress management (including airplane throw) _____

telling your own stories    _____

hearing others' stories    _____

bringing/talking about symbol of person who died _____

icebreaker ABC game    _____

If you were planning the group, what would you add or change?

_____

_____

_____

Thanks for taking the time to share with us. We really enjoyed working with you. Before turning in this evaluation, please tear off at the dotted line and save the information below.

-----------------------------------------------------------------------------------------

(Names and phone numbers of leaders)

(Number of local hotline:            )

**Figure 13.1, page 2.** Sample evaluation #1.

**Evaluation #2**

# TEEN GRIEF GROUP—(HOSPICE SERVICES)

It is helpful for planning future groups to know what worked.

Did you like:

1. time we met_____

2. place we met  _____

3. number of persons in group  _____

4. leaders _____

5. Were the things we talked about and did helpful?

<u>Yes</u>          <u>No</u>

_____       _____       "The Present"

_____       _____       stages of grief

_____       _____       holidays and grief

_____       _____       sharing writings, artwork

---

**Figure 13.2, page 1.** Sample evaluation #2.

<u>Yes</u>        <u>No</u>

_____        _____        talking about conflicts, anger

_____        _____        talking about the person who died

_____        _____        listening to others talk about their person who died

_____        _____        "mirroring"—listening nonverbal exercise

_____        _____        videotape about girl whose dad died

_____        _____        "pound the clay"—releasing that anger

_____        _____        breathing exercise

_____        _____        support system sheet

If you were planning the group, what would you add or change?

Thanks for taking the time to share with us. We really enjoyed working with you. Before turning in this evaluation, please tear off at the dotted line and save the information below.

----------------------------------------------------------------------------------------------------

(Names and phone numbers of leaders)

(Number of local hotline:            )

**Figure 13.2, page 2.** Sample evaluation #2.

**Evaluation #3**

# TEEN GRIEF GROUP—(HOSPICE SERVICES)

It is very helpful for planning future groups to have persons who have participated in a group evaluate it for us. Circle the number that best describes how helpful each of these items was for you.

    1—not very helpful
    2—not helpful
    3—okay
    4—moderately helpful
    5—very helpful

| | | | | | |
|---|---|---|---|---|---|
| 1. Learning about grief and how it affects us | 1 | 2 | 3 | 4 | 5 |
| 2. The chance to talk about the person who died | 1 | 2 | 3 | 4 | 5 |
| 3. Talking about changes in our lives | 1 | 2 | 3 | 4 | 5 |
| 4. Hearing others talk about their experiences | 1 | 2 | 3 | 4 | 5 |
| 5. Being with other teens who had someone die | 1 | 2 | 3 | 4 | 5 |
| 6. Learning how to take better care of myself: "The Present," "Achieving a Balance" | 1 | 2 | 3 | 4 | 5 |
| 7. Writing to the person who died (and how we would like them to respond) | 1 | 2 | 3 | 4 | 5 |

**Figure 13.3, page 1.** Sample evaluation #3.

8. Drawing about our experience of grief      1   2   3   4   5

9. Discussion about preparing for the holidays      1   2   3   4   5

10. Chance to talk about how the holidays went      1   2   3   4   5

11. Talking about supports in my life      1   2   3   4   5

12. Snacks      1   2   3   4   5

13. In general, how helpful was the group?      1   2   3   4   5

What was most helpful about the group?

What was least helpful about the group?

If you were planning the group, what would you add or change?

Thanks for taking the time to share with us. We really enjoyed working with you. Before turning in this evaluation, please tear off at the dotted line and save the information below.

------------------------------------------------------------------------------------------------

(Names and phone numbers of leaders)

(Number of local hotline:       )

**Figure 13.3, page 2.** Sample evaluation #3.

# Chapter 14

# PROVIDING FOLLOW-UP

For many teens, the group is just a beginning—a time to reflect upon the grieving process in a safe environment. They have bonded with others who have embarked upon a similar process. Encourage additional contact among members after the group has formally ended. Some suggestions are given. Leaders are encouraged to expand upon these ideas to develop the right plan for their particular group.

An essential role of the leader is to identify when a teen needs the help of a mental health professional in order to heal the pain of the loss. The section, "How to Determine When Additional Help Is Needed," highlights the "red flags" for a potential suicide and when a leader ought to make a recommendation for professional intervention.

## BEYOND THE GROUP MEETINGS

Often, after the group has ended, the teens or their parents have described how the teens miss getting together with their peers to talk about loss.

A simple phone call is a way to show the teens that they are not forgotten. It is a good opportunity to see if the teen still has an adequate support group or if the situation would warrant the involvement of a mental health professional. Teens who have been seeing a therapist may need some encouragement to continue seeing one. Other teens may need medical care because of constant upset stomachs or sleeping or eating problems, and should be encouraged to seek help. If the person who died was the primary caretaker, another person who now has the caregiver role may be oblivious to signs of a teen needing professional help.

Encourage the teens to call others on the roster list that they received during the sessions. Often the teens have some common threads that bind them. They can be valuable resources for one another.

The leaders can decide how often to phone each teen, whether each month, every three months, or every six months. Make sure that the teens have phone numbers of the leaders, hotline emergency numbers, and other local resources such as mental health clinics.

## Peer Facilitators

If another grief group is beginning, the leader could invite one or two teens from the last group to join the new group. Give details to the last group members about the new group. Some teens may be ready to become peer facilitators. These teens could lead some of the welcoming activities. This gives them a chance to belong to the support group and continue to address their own grief by participating in the activities while encouraging the new members.

When teens have come back for a couple of sets of sessions, they may take even a greater leadership role within the group by assisting with the planning for future groups. When a teen is waiting for a group to begin, the leader can ask a peer facilitator to call and talk about what to expect from the group. Along with the leaders, the peer facilitator can make follow-up calls once the group has ended. This involvement presupposes a high level of maturity, along with additional training. In their training, they need to learn about the "red flags" for teens who may be considering suicide. Peer facilitators need to have access to the leaders for consultation. Working in conjunction with the leaders, peer facilitators can be a wonderful asset for the group, even as they continue to process their own grief.

# HOW TO DETERMINE WHEN ADDITIONAL HELP IS NEEDED

Does a certain teen need more help than the group can provide? From the first interview through the last session, the leaders need to ask this question about each teen. The teen group is not a substitute for psychotherapy or professional counseling.

As a matter of fact, as teens begin to learn about grief and talk about how it is affecting their daily lives, related problems and concerns may surface that require the services of a mental health professional. This additional support could complement the benefits of the group in helping certain teens move through their grief in a healing way.

The following are a few examples of when a referral is needed. Consider these instances and always be asking yourself if one of the group members needs the additional assistance. If so, make the referral or obtain the additional support.

## Suicide Potential—Cues

There are numerous "red flags" to look for in identifying a person at risk for suicide. Robert G. Stevenson (1990) compiled a list in "Teen Suicide: Sources, Signal, and Prevention," a chapter from the book, *The Dying and Bereaved Teenager:*

- a previous attempt;
- abuse of alcohol, drugs;
- talking about suicide;

- loss of appetite, weight, interest in life;
- sudden calm after a long or deep depression;
- giving away possessions;
- obtaining a gun, collecting pills;
- creative works that show recurrent themes of depression, death or "pressure"; and
- a sudden change in almost any recurring pattern of behavior. (Stevenson, 1990, pp. 129–130)

If the leader observes these characteristics, not in isolation but as part of a pattern of behaviors, it would be well to discuss it with a mental health professional to determine if it is a threatening situation. The parent may need to be contacted. Tell the teen about your concern. It is necessary to waive confidentiality and talk with a parent.

If the teen is in immediate danger of committing suicide, a "suicide watch" may be necessary. Then, an adult stays with the teen while a parent or an emergency person whom the parent designated on the registration form is contacted. The teen is not left alone. Stay with the teen until the designated person arrives. An emergency plan is made, and the teen remains supervised until help is secured.

Stevenson wrote, "For a person considering suicide, suicide is not a problem, it is a solution. The person not so much wishes 'to be dead', but to be relieved of some pressure, pain, or problem that they can no longer face" (1990, p. 127). Relief from that intense pain requires the concentrated effort of a skilled professional along with the support of family and friends.

During a grief group, however, teens routinely will talk about their outbursts of anger, episodes of depression, or thoughts of suicide. This is an opportunity for leaders to emphasize what steps teens can take when suicidal thoughts persist. Remind the teens that it is necessary to talk to others, particularly adults, to move through the intense feelings. Provide them with the phone number of a crisis hotline, the leaders' numbers, and other numbers where mental health services are available.

## Grieving More Than One Loss

The director of a hospice received a phone call from the local veterinarian who was concerned about a woman who was devastated when her dog was hit by a truck. The vet had called the hospice office because the woman talked non-stop about her daughter who had died of cancer three years earlier. The loss of the dog had triggered the fear, the sadness, and even the anger of losing her only daughter at the young age of 49. In another example, a parent's death may revive the pain of a sibling's death or the divorce that resulted in the upheaval of moving away from the other parent, friends, and schools.

The teen may be grieving the fluffy dog who helped the teen endure the long painful dying of his dad but cannot move to the apartment in the new city where the bereaved mom has found a decent paying job.

Many changes can result from the death of a main caregiver. Each loss needs to be grieved. This can require more time and individual attention than is available in a group. A mental health professional can provide that kind of support.

## Unresolved Conflicts

The relationship with the deceased may have been in conflict at the time of death. There may be guilt issues too deeply imbedded or too sensitive to be shared in a group. A counselor or spiritual guide may need to be consulted.

## Limited Support System

Often a death in the family creates havoc upon the family equilibrium. Some parents refuse to mention the name of the deceased. They attempt to go on as if nothing happened. The children pick up the message, "It is not okay to grieve in this house."

In some instances, a bereaved parent is so overwhelmed with grief that the parent cannot provide the support and encouragement the child needs in order that he or she can deal with the grief experience.

When steady support is absent, a teen may need to find a professional who can help explore the many dimensions of grief over time. Activity 12.1, "Supports in My Life," can help teens examine the extent of their support systems. If the quality of support is limited, professional help should be recommended.

# RESOURCE MATERIAL

## Books for Adults and Older Teens

Bernstein, Joanne. (1977). *Loss and how to cope with it*. New York: Seabury Press.

Bernstein, Joanne, & Masha Kabahow Reedman. (1989). *Books to help children cope with separation and loss: An annotated bibliography*. New York: R.R. Bowker.

Bode, Janet. (1994). *Death is hard to live with*. New York: Delacorte.

Cole, Diane. (1992). *After great pain, a new life emerges*. New York: Summit Books.

Donnelly, Katherine Fair. (1988). *Recovering from the loss of a sibling*. New York: Dodd, Mead and Company.

Donnelly, Katherine Fair. (1993). *Recovering from the loss of a parent*. New York: Berkley Publishing Group.

Fox, Sandra. (1985). *Good grief: helping groups of children when a friend dies*. Boston: New England Association for Education of Young Children.

Grollman, Earl A. (1993). *Straight talk about death for teenagers*. Boston: Beacon Press.

Jewett, Claudia. (1983). *Helping children cope with separation and loss*. Grand Rapids, MI: Zondervan Publishing House.

Kubler-Ross, Elisabeth. (1969). *On death and dying*. New York: Macmillan Publishing Company.

Kubler-Ross, Elisabeth. (1982). *Working it through*. New York: Macmillan Publishing Company.

Lord, Janice Harris. (1987). *No time for good-byes: Coping with sorrow, anger and injustice after a tragic death.* Ventura, CA: Pathfinder Publishing.

Lord, Janice Harris. (1992). *Beyond sympathy: What to say and do for someone suffering an injury, illness or loss.* Ventura, CA: Pathfinder Publishing.

Merritt, Stephanie. (1996). *Mind, music, and imagery: Unlocking your creative potential* (2nd ed.). Santa Rosa, CA: Aslan Publishing.

Miller, Jack. (1993). *Healing our losses: a journal for working through your grief.* San Jose, CA: Resource Publications.

Oates, Wayne Edward. (1981). *Your particular grief.* Philadelphia: Westminster Press.

O'Brien, Mauryeen. (1993). *The new day journal.* New Rochelle, NY: Don Bosco Multimedia.

Schneider, John. (1984). *Stress, loss, and grief.* Baltimore: University Park Press.

Stearns, Ann Kaiser. (1984). *Living through personal crisis.* New York: Ballantine Books.

Stearns, Ann Kaiser. (1988). *Coming back: Rebuilding lives after crisis and loss.* New York: Random House Publishers.

Tatelbaum, Judy. (1980). *The courage to grieve.* New York: Harper and Row Publishers.

Viorst, Judith. (1986). *Necessary losses.* New York: Simon and Schuster.

Wolf, Anthony E. (1991). *Get out of my life, but first could you drive me and Cheryl to the mall: A parent's guide to the new teenager.* New York: Noonday Press.

Worden, J. William. (1991). *Grief counseling and grief therapy: A handbook for the mental health practitioner.* New York: Springer Publishing Company.

Worden, J. William. (1995). *When a parent dies: Counseling bereaved children.* New York: Guilford Press.

## Related Articles and Pamphlets

Boyd, Cynthia. (1980, June 20). Groups help the grieving through pain. *Boca Raton News*.

Carey, Anne L., Della Copeland, & Rik Cryderman. (1992, Fall). The rituals of life that say we belong. *Thanatos, 17,* 13–14.

Cottle, Tom. (1982). When a parent dies. *Highwire, 2*(3), 43–47. (transcript from a television show)

George, Annette. (1984, Winter). Groups make good grief. *Interaction* (newsletter of the Association for Religious and Value Issues in Counseling), *2,* 1–3.

Gray, Ross E. (1988). The role of school counselors with bereaved teenagers: With and without peer support groups. *The School Counselor, 35*(3), 185–193.

Gray, Ross E. (1989). Adolescents' perceptions of social support after the death of a parent. *Journal of Psychosocial Oncology, 7*(3), 127–144.

Jacobsen, Gail B. (1990). *Write grief: How to transform loss with writing.* Menomonee Falls, WI: McCormick and Schilling.

Kandt, Victoria. (1994). Adolescent bereavement: Turning a fragile time into acceptance and peace. *The School Counselor, 41*(3), 203–211.

Masterman, Sharon Hale, & Redmond Reams. 1988. Support groups for bereaved preschool and school-age children. *American Journal of Orthopsychiatry, 58*(4), 562–570.

McMahon, Edwin M., & Peter A. Campbell. (1991). *The focusing steps.* Missouri: Sheed and Ward.

Moore, Julia. (1992). When your friend's parent dies. *Thanatos, 17*(2), 10–11.

Oltjenbruns, Kevin Ann. (1991). Positive outcomes of adolescents' experience with grief. *Journal of Adolescent Research, 6*(1), 43–53.

Perschy, Mary K. (1988). Teen grief group: Respite from isolation. *Bereavement Magazine, 4*(5), 42–43.

Perschy, Mary K. (1989, Winter). Crazy grief. *To Make the Road Less Lonely,* 1& 3.

Powers, Marie. (1981). Is there new life after a parent's death? *Marriage and Family Living, 63*(3), 18–20.

Rosemond, John. (1988, August). When children grieve: Helping them cope with the pain. *Better Homes and Gardens,* (26), 31.

Scravani, Mark. (1992). *When death walks in.* Omaha: Centering Corporation.

Stevenson, Robert G. (1990). Teen suicide: Sources, signals, and prevention. In John Morgan (Ed.), *The dying and bereaved teenager* (pp. 125–139). New York: The Charles Press, Publishers.

Tekulve, Louise. (1992, December). The seasons of grief. *Bereavement Magazine, 6,* 12. Colorado Springs: Bereavement Publishing.

Traisman, Enid. (1993). *Fire in my heart, ice in my veins.* Omaha: Centering Corporation.

Tubesing, Nancy, & Donald Tubesing. (1983). "Goodbye" means ouch! *The Stress Examiner.* Duluth, Minnesota: Whole Person Associates, in cooperation with Aid Association for Lutherans.

Williams, Katie. (1992, October). No where to run. *Bereavement Magazine, 6,* 12–13. Colorado Springs: Bereavement Publishing.

Wolfelt, Alan. (1987, Winter). Resolution versus reconciliation: The importance of semantics. *Thanatos, 12,* 10–13.

Wolfelt, Alan. (1988, Spring). Reconciliation needs of the mourner: Reworking a critical concept in caring for the bereaved. *Thanatos. 13,* 6–10.

## Materials That Include the Spiritual Aspects

Hewett, John H. (1980). *After suicide.* Philadelphia: The Westminster Press.

Krauss, Pesach, & Morrie Goldfischer. (1988). *Why me?: Coping with grief, loss, and change.* New York: Bantam Books.

Kuenning, Delores. (1987). *Helping people through grief.* Minneapolis: Bethany House Publishers.

Kushner, Harold S. (1981). *When bad things happen to good people.* New York: Avon Books.

Manning, Doug. 1984. *Don't take my grief away: What to do when you lose a loved one.* New York: Harper and Row Publishers.

Nouwen, Henri J.M. (1982). *A letter of consolation.* New York: Harper Collins Publishers.

Wolff, Pierre. (1979). *May I hate God?* New York: Paulist Press.

## Books Specifically Related to Teen Grief (Non-fiction)

Graville, Karen, & Charles Haskins. (1989). *Teenagers face to face with bereavement.* Englewood Cliffs, NJ: Julian Messner.

Krementz, Jill. (1981). *How it feels when a parent dies.* New York: Knopf Publishing Company.

Le Shan, Eda. (1976). *Learning to say goodbye: When a parent dies.* New York: Macmillan Publishing Company.

Richter, Elizabeth. (1986). *Losing someone you love: When a brother or sister dies.* New York: G.P. Putnam's Sons.

Schaefer, Dan, & Christine Lyons. (1986). *How do we tell the children?* New York: Newmarket Press.

## Books Specifically Related to Teen Grief (Fiction)

Blume, Judy. (1981). *Tiger eyes.* New York: Dell Publishing Company.

Mann, Peggy. (1977). *There are two kinds of terrible.* Garden City, NY: Doubleday Press.

Paterson, Katherine. (1977). *Bridge to Terabitha.* New York: Crowell Publishing Company.

## Children's Books That Could Be Used with Young and Old

Buscalgia, Leo. (1982). *The fall of Freddie the leaf*. Bellmawr, NJ: Holt, Rinehart, and Winston.

Sanford, Doris. (1985). *It must hurt a lot*. Portland: Multnomah Press.

Smith, Doris Buchanan. (1973). *A taste of blackberries*. New York: Harper and Row Junior Books.

Varley, Susan. (1984). *Badger's parting gifts*. New York: Lothrop.

Viorst, Judith. (1971). *The 10th good thing about Barney*. New York: Athenenum.

## Additional Resources

Bio-Spiritual Focusing Regional Program (as developed by Edwin M. McMahon, Ph.D., & Peter A. Campbell, Ph.D.). For information and a newsletter, write or call: Loretta Flom, Bio-Spiritual Research, P.O. Box 741137, Arvada, CO 80006-1137, Telephone/FAX: 303-427-5311.

Grief Art Project. For information write: Carol Lobell, 10523 Tolling Clock Way, Columbia, MD 21044. This project shows stages of grief in a graphic form, and is available in various sizes.

# REFERENCES

Fox, S. (1988). *Good grief: Helping groups of children when a friend dies.* Boston: New England Association for the Education of Young Children.

Gray, R. E. (1988, March). The role of school counselors with bereaved teenagers: With and without peer support groups. *The School Counselor, 35,* 185–193.

Jacobsen, G. B. (1990). *Write grief: How to transform loss with writing.* Menomonee Falls, WI: McCormick and Schilling.

Kubler-Ross, E. (1969). *On death and dying.* New York: Macmillan Publishing Company.

McMahon, E., & Campbell, P. A. (1991). *The focusing steps.* Kansas City: Sheed and Ward.

Merritt, S. (1996). *Mind, music, and imagery: Unlocking your creative potential.* Santa Rosa, CA: Aslan Publishing.

Oltjenbruns, K. A. (1991). Positive outcomes of adolescents' experience with grief. *Journal of Adolescent Research, 6*(1), 43–53.

Perschy, M. K. (1989, Winter). Crazy grief. *To Make the Road Less Lonely,* 1 & 3 (newsletter).

Stevenson, R. G. (1990). Teen suicide: Sources, signals, and prevention. In J. Morgan (Ed), *The dying and bereaved teenager* (pp. 125–139). New York: The Charles Press, Publishers.

Tatelbaum, J. (1980). *The courage to grieve.* New York: HarperCollins Publishers.

Williams, K. (1992, October). No where to run. *Bereavement Magazine,* 12–13.

Wolf, A. E. (1991). *Get out of my life, but first could you drive me and Cheryl to the mall: A parent's guide to the new teenager.* New York: Noonday Press.

Wolfelt, A. (1987, Winter). Resolution versus reconciliation: The importance of semantics. *Thanatos, 12,* 10–13.

Worden, J. W. (1991). *Grief counseling and grief therapy* (2nd ed.). New York: Springer Publishing Company.

# INDEX

## ABOUT THE AUTHOR

Over the years, ***Mary Kelly Perschy, M.S.,*** has acquired a healthy regard for the process of grief. She has worked with grieving teens for over 10 years and is convinced that the support of caring adults accelerates the healing process when teens are willing to wrestle with their grief.

A graduate of Trocaire and Medaille colleges in Buffalo, New York, and Johns Hopkins University in Baltimore, Maryland, Perschy has served as teacher, administrator, and counselor. Currently she is Bereavement Coordinator at Hospice Services of Howard County in Columbia, Maryland.

She lives with her husband, Jim, and son and daughter in Maryland.